KT-451-151

English Plus

A practical scheme of work for the examination years

T McSweeney
St Peter's High School, Prestwich

M Elam
Ellen Wilkinson High School, Manchester

with additional material by

R Scrowston
St Brendan's Sixth Form College, Bristol

J P Murphy
St Peter's High School, Prestwich

LONGMAN

Scheme of work

Introduction

This book is a result of a need expressed by a large number of teachers in Secondary and Further Education. At a series of meetings of English teachers held in different parts of the country, the teachers were asked about their external examination classes in English language. More than three-quarters said that they spent a considerable portion of the fifth year going through past papers. More than half expressed uncertainty as to the criteria adopted by the examiners and the levels of the grades. Teachers in Further Education said that this was particularly important for their evening class or day release students who probably saw their teacher only once a week. There was another factor: the large number of teachers who were teaching English language, but were not trained to do so. The four teachers involved in this book have more than forty years' experience of examining English.

The work is of a standard suitable for the O level, 16[+] and new combined examination. It is primarily suitable for the written examination but can be used for continuous assessment. It gives widespread practice in the major areas that all the Examining Boards stipulate in their syllabuses. It gives indication of what the examiners are looking for and, for those students and teachers who want help, it suggests methods of approach and marking schemes. Chapters on vocabulary and punctuation are included, not because they are examined as such nowadays but because (*a*) insufficient attention to the implication of words is a major reason for low marks in comprehension questions, and (*b*) faulty punctuation consistently brings down the mark for the essay. There is a different approach to punctuation stressing what the writer wants to achieve rather than rules regarding different stops. This has been developed from a recommendation put forward in *Language Across the Curriculum*.

Words in their context

Words are the beginning. Whether we want to appreciate the writing of others or to develop our own writing we must begin with words. As children, we speak as children; as we grow older our ideas, feelings and reactions develop and become more complex and we need words and vocabulary to express this development. We need to learn to love words, to be fascinated by the sound of words, by the shape and feel and appeal of words. We need to learn how words say things directly, but also how they hint, half-create, suggest and reach deep down into our minds. In order to realise how they do this we need to know first how words work.

How words work

Mainly functional words

Some words have quite specific or definite meanings associated with them: e.g. oxygen, algebra (these are known as lexis or lexical words).

Others have more of a function than a meaning: e.g. if, when, should. These tend to be short and often monosyllabic words and in the ten most frequently used words in the language they are the majority. These ten are: the, of, and, to, a, in, with, it, is, I.

In spite of their shortness these words often control and determine completely the meaning of a statement. If the lexical words are the bricks of a sentence or a language, then the functional words are the cement, mortar, hinges, etc. which bring the bricks together into a quite definite relationship.

The following pairs of sentences may be joined in a number of ways: by adding although, but, etc.

Write out each pair of sentences joined together in as many ways as you can and explain the implication of each sentence.

1 He was poor/he was honest.
2 He played for United/he was a good player.

In the following sentences a function word has been left out. See how many words you can supply for each sentence and explain how each word gives a slightly different meaning to the sentence.

3 The doctor _____ come at 2.00 p.m.
4 Who _____ help those people in distress?

The importance of these function words will be dealt with at greater length in the notes on the comprehension of a passage of writing.

Words with meanings

In fact, relatively few words have a definite meaning in the way the word *oxygen* has. Most words have meanings which vary from a slight to a considerable degree according to the context in which they are used. It is often not possible to give the meaning of a word in isolation. It is no more possible to do so than it is to say whether twenty years, for example, is a long time. It is sometimes not even possible to say how a word is pronounced if all we are given is the word: e.g. wound, wind, bow, compact, content.

If we cannot say how a word is pronounced out of context how much more difficult to say what the meaning of a word is out of context.

Reference and association

However, we can recognise two elements in the meanings of most words. Consider the two adjectives: **maternal   motherly**
A dictionary defines them as follows:

maternal – of or pertaining to a mother/maternal. Related through the mother.
motherly – of or characteristic of a mother. Having the qualities suitable in a mother; for example, tenderness or affectionate solicitude.

a) What do these two words have in common?
b) What difference is there between them?
c) Are they interchangeable?
d) Compose sentences using each word and then transpose the word into the other sentence. How is the meaning changed? Are the words used properly in the new sentence?

We may take as another example the two nouns: **steed   horse**
Ask the same questions for them as were asked for **maternal** and **motherly**. The answers to both sets of questions will show that there are two elements in the meanings of these words.

First there is what the word refers to, sometimes called the reference value of the word. We can also call it the dictionary definition of the word. Although 'steed' originally meant a horse or stallion it is altogether different from the word 'horse'. Most people associate it with knights, armour, romance. Similarly maternal and motherly have quite different associations. This part of the meaning of a word is sometimes called the emotive or associative content.

Changed meaning Words can often change their meaning rapidly because of what they are associated with: e.g. **chauvinism**

Even a modern dictionary gives the following meaning:

chauvinism – exaggerated and aggressive patriotism (from Nicholas Chauvin, a devoted adherent of Napoleon Bonaparte).

Here we can see how a particular usage, i.e. male chauvinism, has completely changed the meaning of a word. Although many people (and this unfortunately includes many of the people who set examinations in English for the Examination Boards) object to such changes in meaning they are part of the healthy development of a flourishing language.

Whether we are reading what has been written by others or expressing our own ideas and feelings in words, we constantly need to be aware of the full range of meaning of the words used.

This awareness is something which can be learnt, particularly by studying words in and out of their context and by experimenting with them in and out of context.

Exercises

1 The following words have a basic meaning of giving out light:
twinkle, glow, sparkle, shine, flash, gleam, glare, glisten, glint, dazzle, scintillate, glitter, glimmer, shimmer, coruscate, flicker.

a) Analyse the meaning of each of the words under the following headings:

Word	Type of light	Steadiness of light	Special associations
Glare	Harsh	Steady	A context of hurting or anger

b) Give each verb some common subject: e.g. 'His eyes . . . ' and explain what the verb suggests in this context.

2 Consider the following groups of words in a similar manner:
a) digress, deviate, swerve, veer, diverge, meander
b) fluent, talkative, glib, loquacious, garrulous, long-winded, flippant
c) pale, pallid, pasty, faded, wan, sallow
d) recruit, apprentice, novice, probationer, debutante
e) whisper, mutter, murmur, mumble
f) habit, tradition, vogue, fad, obsession, custom

Emotive use of language

Some words appeal more to our emotions and feelings rather than to our reason. Consider: **crowd   mob**

Both words refer to a gathering of people, but whereas crowd is fairly neutral in tone, mob definitely has unpleasant associations.

In addition, the use of the word indicates the attitude of the speaker towards the crowd of people and consequently the use of the word 'mob' is intended to influence and determine the attitude of the reader or listener towards the group of people. We will tend to think badly of them whether it is justified or not.

At its best the emotive use of language creates powerful reading; at its worst it is the language of hatred, of racial, religious and political intolerance. It is frequently the language of advertising.

Exercises

1 The following lines, when unravelled, present four versions of a section from an estate agent's house description. The versions differ according to the emotive tone established by the words/phrases chosen from each of the sets of four alternatives. Version A gives an extremely favourable impression of the property; version B gives milder praise; version C is uncomplimentary; version D would probably ensure that the house was never sold.

After careful reading and discussion to identify the two extreme versions (A and D) write out what in your opinion best represents version B and version C.

This (pleasant, squalid, mean, exclusive) (residence, abode, slum, dwelling) was (built, constructed, assembled, thrown up) (within the last decade, ten years back, only ten years since, approximately ten years ago) and has (of late, more recently, in the interim, since) been (crudely, gradually, occasionally, meticulously) (extended, enlarged, built out, added to) by the present (occupiers, tenants, inhabitants, owners) (to create, to provide, resulting in, producing) a (comfortable, shambolic, haphazard, splendid) family home. It (gives, affords, offers, amounts to) (ill-, well-, marvellously, carelessly) planned and (compact, deceptively roomy, poky, cramped) (habitation, living quarters, accommodation, living space), (neatly, sumptuously, tastelessly, casually) decorated and (barely, shoddily, immaculately, conscientiously) maintained. (Ugly, Attractive, Unsightly, Inviting) gardens further (complement, lend to, mar, detract from) the appearance of the (property, hovel, premises, place), and there is considerable (scope, room, opportunity, potential) for (further extension, imaginative development, necessary alterations, improvement). The house is (poorly sited, conveniently positioned, unfortunately located, ideally situated) being (virtually adjacent to, practically isolated from, within easy walking distance of, within reach of) most local amenities.

2 The following is taken from a very ornate menu:
Succulent strips of hand-picked beef lightly brushed in fragrant fine herbs and expertly fried in butter to your own specification, smothered in a mouthwatering mushroom sauce and accompanied by fresh, naturally grown peas.

a) This is in fact quite an ordinary preparation of food. Pick out the words or phrases which make the food and the preparation seem better than it probably was.
b) Draw up another example of an ordinary meal and describe it in similar terms.
c) Write a short description of a school that was trying to attract parents to send their children to it.
d) Write another description of the same school by a pupil who did not like it. The description should follow point by point that in the official description.

3 Arrange the following groups of words according to the categories indicated below:
Show strong dislike   Mild dislike   Neutral
Favourable towards   Very favourable towards

a) crowd, mob, congregation, audience, gathering
b) fat, plump, obese, overweight, corpulent, heavy
c) dull, listless, uninteresting, boring, colourless
d) slim, slender, skinny, bony, thin
e) hasty, decisive, rash, quick, fast, headstrong, reckless
f) solemn, serious, earnest, humourless
g) bright, vivid, gaudy, glaring, garish, colourful
h) The words contained in examples b), c), f) on page 8.

Using dictionaries

After the Bible, dictionaries are the best selling categories of books. It is estimated that more than 60 per cent of households have at least one dictionary in them. There are various types of dictionaries. The most common are those that deal with the meanings of words, but there are also dictionaries of people, of places (a gazetteer) and technical or specialised dictionaries, such as a medical dictionary, a dictionary of sporting terms, a dictionary of the arts. In addition there are encyclopaedias which may deal with people, places, and words, but which are intended to be more comprehensive in their range. Many modern dictionaries are encyclopaedic dictionaries, that is, although they are mainly concerned with words they include information on prominent people and places. Two such extremely useful dictionaries are *Longman Modern English Dictionary*, and the *Encyclopedia Dictionary* published by Hamlyn.

Here is an example from an entry in a modern dictionary:

> **Ice** (ais) 1. *n.* water solidified by freezing ‖ the frozen surface of water ‖ (*Br.*) a portion of ice cream ‖ (esp. *Am.*) a sweet of frozen, sweetened water flavoured with fruit juice etc. ‖ something looking like ice, *camphor ice* TO BREAK THE ICE to break down the formality or reserve in human intercourse ‖ to be the first of a group to do some group action TO CUT NO ICE to be ineffective, make no impression TO SKATE (or BE or TREAD) ON THIN ICE to be dealing with a matter where there is great danger of making a mistake or causing personal offence unless great care is taken. 2. *v. pres. part.* ICING *v.t.* to convert into ice ‖ to cover with ice ‖ to cool by adding or applying ice to or by refrigerating, *to ice beer* ‖ to cover with icing, *to ice a cake* ‖ *v.i.* to become coated with ice [O.E. *is*]

Longman Modern English Dictionary

Organisation of dictionaries

In order to get the best use out of the dictionary it is extremely important to understand how it is organised.

1 **The information at the front of the dictionary** is important as it will explain the organisation of the dictionary. There is also generally a list of abbreviations used, phonetic symbols, or the particular use of typographical aids such as round brackets ( ), the double oblique line ‖, and what is known as the swung dash, ~.

2 **Alphabetical arrangements**. The words are generally arranged alphabetically and although this seems self-explanatory there are one or two points which need to be considered.

   a) Alternative spellings – generally these are under the alphabetical arrangement for the most common spelling, e.g. humour.

   b) Derivations. If a word is derived from the main word being considered, it may be included under that word or it may be in its alphabetical order, e.g. humorous. If this word was taken alphabetically it would appear before humour in an English dictionary.

   c) We need to establish whether names beginning with Mac or St occur in the alphabetical order.

3 **Head word or catch word**. This is a word printed in a bolder (heavier) type at the head of an entry in the dictionary, e.g. the word **Ice** in the above example. In some dictionaries in order to avoid the repetition of the head word, either a dash (or the swung dash) is used to indicate the head word.

4 a) **The different meanings** are generally numbered. In the above example the double line is used.

   b) The most common, modern meaning is generally given first. However, the Oxford Dictionary is organised on historical principles, that is, it gives the earliest meaning of the words and progresses in chronological order.

   c) Expressions and idioms using the head word are then generally given as in the above example – to break the ice.

5 **Pronunciation**. The guide to the symbols used is given at the front of the dictionary or sometimes at the bottom of the page. Most dictionaries also indicate which consonants are stressed or accentuated. Alternative pronunciations should also be given.

6 **Parts of speech**. The same word may be used as a different part of speech, e.g. 'ice' can be both a noun or a verb. The dictionary should indicate how the word may be used as a different part of speech.

7 **Types of usage (including register)**. Although the meaning of the word may be quite clear, in fact its usage may be confined to a particular type of speech. The dictionary should indicate this, as for example: colloquial, slang, obsolete, archaic, vulgar, Americanism. Often the dictionary will give an illustration of the usage.

8 **Etymology**. The dictionaries will give you the origin of the word and you are often able to see how it has altered its meaning to arrive at its present meaning.

Dictionary exercises

1 The meanings of the following words can be extended by adding to them other words (prepositions), e.g. put – put out, put over, put up with. These produce fine shades of meaning which can be confusing. For each of the following words write out as many extended versions as you can and then from each list select 3 examples and explain how the added word(s) has changed the meaning:

put, give, come, go, get, bring

2 Distinguish between 'to hang up' and 'to hang down'.

3 Use a dictionary to find out the pronunciation and alternative pronunciations of the following words:

wound, bow, controversy, schedule, distribute, scone

4 Use a dictionary to find the origin of the following words:

silly, sad, treacle, style, salary, dress, child, girl

5 If you are watching an American film or reading an American novel, you could quite easily come across the following words. Find out what is the common English equivalent of them:

sidewalk, suspenders, apartment, faucet

6 The following words have more than one meaning. Arrange them in order beginning with the meaning you think is the most common and ending with the least common:

pad, school, fine, go, will, open, hand, bat, nice

7 Use the dictionary to find out the particular circumstances in which the following words are used in a non-standard way:

lousy, nonce, fabulous, diamond, intern, brat, posh

8 *Definitions*: define clearly the meaning of each word in the following groups. Write one sentence for each definition.

a) audible, tumultuous, vociferous
b) departure, divergence, detour
c) consequence, pre-condition, symptom
d) emphatic, indefinite, precise
e) simile, metaphor, personification
f) alliteration, assonance, onomatopoeia
g) contrary, amenable, equivocal
h) convey, evoke, elaborate (verb)
i) ironic, sarcastic, sardonic
j) exhilaration, stimulation, provocation

9 Words clarified by their context: for each of the following pairs of words compose two sentences to show that you understand the difference in meaning between the words in each pair.

impotent/impudent	practice/practise
affected/effected	ingenious/ingenuous
dependent/dependant	implicate/implicit
ineligible/intelligible	stationary/stationery
precede/proceed	licence/license
persecute/prosecute	innate/insight
illimitable/inimitable	compliment/complement
access/excess	allusion/illusion
elicit/illicit	disapprove/disprove
ensure/insure	immunity/impunity

Using a thesaurus

A thesaurus is a vocabulary where words of related meaning are categorised by topics and backed by an alphabetical index to show you where to look for whatever shade of meaning you require.

At this stage it is a more useful tool than a dictionary, especially for those moments in writing where you are aware of what you want to say but can't quite grasp the word that will best express it.

For example, you suddenly need a different way to state the word 'overall', in order to avoid repeating the word in an essay or to paraphrase it in answering a comprehension question. Turning to the index of the thesaurus, you discover:

overall – inclusive 78 adj.
      apron 228 noun
      trousers 228 noun

As the synonym (i.e. word of similar meaning) that you require concerns 'inclusiveness', rather than clothing, turn to category (*not* page) 78 and find the subdivision which lists adjectives. Immediately you have several alternatives from which to select the word most suited to your context: total, all embracing, comprehensive, universal, etc.

Now tackle these exercises to familiarise yourself with the handling of a thesaurus.

Exercises

1 An exercise in direct speech demands alternatives for 'he said'. Refer to 'say' and 'talk' in the index and find a dozen other options. Use a dictionary to check on shades of difference in meaning of the words that you select.

2 You are conscious of over-using the following words. Find substitutes.

suddenly (refer to synonyms for sudden, adj.)
eventually   enormous   delicious   small
great   horrible

3 You need words more specific than:

walk (slowly)   smell (foul)
hot (extremely)   eat (speedily/crudely)

4 Find a synonym for each of the following:

exaggerated	mischievous
circumspect	technique
feasible	contrast
transfer	itemise
gesticulate	next
supernatural	grateful
popular	request
description	forgive
superficial	perpetual
inferior	memorable
enhance	conclusion
loquacious	condense

15

Registers

Consider the following:

SHUT UP
CLOSE YOUR TRAP
BE QUIET
WOULD YOU KINDLY MAKE LESS NOISE

Although all of these give the same message, they are very different in tone, manner, effect, and almost certainly will receive a different type of response.

Which of them would be appropriate or totally inappropriate for the following to use?

1 A clergyman at the start of his sermon.
2 A nurse speaking to noisy visitors in a hospital ward.
3 A shop manager trying to calm down complaining customers.

What do you think would be the response of an inappropriate choice for each of the above?

How do you think the following would ask for quiet?

1 An official introducing a member of the royalty.
2 A teacher with a noisy class of infants.
3 A teacher with a noisy class of teenagers seeing the headteacher approaching the classroom.
4 A pupil to an unattended class seeing the headteacher approach.

All of the above give examples of different registers of language.

Register refers to the appropriateness of the language used for a particular occasion. It includes choice of words, expressions, sentence construction and, in spoken English, tone, emphasis and articulation. As the examples above show, what is appropriate in one situation may be very inappropriate for another.

Examiners' reports constantly refer to choice of inappropriate registers in essays and letters. The candidate has to distinguish between situations where a use of formal, semi-formal or informal (i.e. colloquial) English is required. But even within these broad groups there may be appropriate and inappropriate registers, e.g. a letter to a friend in which you have to tell him tactfully of something unwelcome to him will require a more careful choice of words and expressions than a rambling chatty letter to the same friend.

What has made matters a little more difficult is that, in the past, examiners demanded only formal English, but now we recognise that a more colloquial register is acceptable in certain circumstances, e.g. English books regularly said that you should not use I'm – can't, – it's me – for their more formal equivalents, but now their use is not penalised provided it is done intentionally and appropriately to reduce the formal effect.

Exercises

1 Explain the type of situation that the following openings establish:

a) 'Brothers, we've come here to . . .'
b) 'My dear brethren we are gathered together . . .'
c) 'Ladies and Gentlemen . . .'
d) 'Now, you lot . . .'
e) 'Have you heard the one about . . .?'
f) A letter beginning with
   i Dear Sir,
   ii Dear Sir or Madam,
   iii Sir,
   iv Dear Smith,
   v Dear Mrs Smith,
   vi Dear Jim,
   vii My dearest Susan,

2 Write letters to a close friend (of either sex) who takes offence easily:

a) reminding him/her that he has not returned a record of yours.
b) reminding him/her that you have bought at his request something for him and he has not yet paid for it.
c) telling him/her that you are going to a disco with his/her boy/girlfriend who is supposed to be going with the person you are writing to.

3 Write out a conversation between a store detective and a person accused of shop lifting:

a) when the person accused is innocent but the store detective is sure of his/her accusation.
b) when the person accused is guilty but the store detective is not so sure.

4 Think of as many terms of affection as you can: e.g. darling, dearie, love
and explain in what context they are used.

5 Think of as many terms as you can which are used to attract attention: e.g. Hello there!
and say in what context they are used.

6 If you are studying a Shakespeare play, look at Shakespeare's use of register especially between characters of different social levels. Analyse a scene not according to what happens but according to how the characters talk to each other and react to each other, e.g. Falstaff and the Prince in *Henry IV*.

7 Give a brief description of:

a) The registers used within your own family.
b) The registers used amongst your friends.
c) The registers used in any TV domestic comedy.

Special vocabularies

Language is used in order to communicate. If what you want to communicate is information or ideas on a special subject, then you will often have to use words special to that subject. However, you should always aim for two things: CLARITY and ACCURACY.

The following is from the BBC's description of their microcomputer system. It is meant to give information to prospective buyers in the general public.

The non Teletext display modes provide user definable characters in addition to the standard upper and lower case alpha-numeric font.

Even though this may be accurate, it certainly fails from the point of view of clarity. If you are not acquainted with the computer terminology, it could well be a foreign language. Sometimes it is only a matter of vocabulary and your familiarity with it: e.g. wheel, steering-wheel, fly-wheel refer to parts of a car.

Wheel is in general use; *steering-wheel*, although specific to a vehicle, is widely understood and almost self-explanatory; but *fly-wheel* does not explain itself and will probably be understood only by people who have studied engines.

There are two points you should always keep in mind when using or reading technical (i.e. specialised) language:

1 Many words have a general meaning, but can also have technical meanings.
   e.g. mode, clutch, spleen, gear
Make certain that you never confuse the two uses.

2 Some words have a technical sense in one subject and a different technical sense in another subject.
   e.g. solution (in Maths and Chemistry)
   plant (in Botany and Snooker)
Again, these different usages should be clearly understood and not confused.

Exercises

1 The following words have a general and technical meaning, as indicated in the brackets. Bring out the difference in meaning, either by explanation or by using them in sentences: tense (Languages), relief (Geography), string (Computers), forge (Craft), range (Geography), mood (Languages), revolting (History), value (Maths), conductor (Physics), energy (Physics), hardware (Computers), paddle (Computers).

2 The following words have different specialised meanings in the topics indicated. Bring out the different meanings, either by explanation or by using them in sentences:

terminal (Transport, Health, Electricity)
power (Maths, Physics, History)
character (Literature, Typing)
bracket (Craft, Punctuation)
column (Architecture, Printing)
plane (Maths, Craft)
joint (Craft, Cookery)
dissolve (History, Chemistry)
balance (P E, Science, Commerce)
file (Craft, Geography, Commerce, Computer Studies)
plot (Literature, Maths, History)

3 Find out from the subject teacher the ten most important words in the following subjects and show that you understand the full meaning of them:

Geography, History, Languages, Physics, Chemistry, Biology, Art, Domestic Science

4 *Examination vocabulary.* The following words and expressions appear time and time again in examination questions. Show that you understand what is required by each of them:

compare and contrast
discuss
support with references
support with quotations
analyse
examine
give an account of

Jargon

Jargon takes the use of specialised vocabulary one step further. Its purpose often is to exclude people who are not in the know (the word *jargon* originally meant the chattering of birds); e.g. doctors and nurses in conversation with each other could speak about 'sub-orbital haematoma', but if they were talking to non-medical people they should refer to it as a black eye. Even worse is the use of a particular type of jargon which is intended to obscure or avoid stating the truth as in the following parody of a political speech.

'That is a very good question and I am glad you asked it. Just before I go on to answer it I wonder if I may be allowed to refer briefly to something you said earlier, and I would like to make two points about it. First, at this moment in time, when the matter is under active consideration, I think it would be less than helpful if we did not engage in an on-going dialogue which hopefully will produce viable alternatives. Secondly, a meaningful exploration would allow all of us – and by that I mean *all* of us – to maximise the opportunities to re-structure the whole concept of the interface between the Government and schools. Lastly, this calls for the personal involvement of each individual in these interactive processes which are the lifeblood of our democracy. And· finally, the whole country has to pull together as a team, and when things go wrong – as they can for even the best of teams – we are not to let our heads sink, but we have to knock it around a little and run for each other, for that is what it is all about. Could I have the next question please?'

Exercises

1 Express the following examples of jargon in simpler terms:

at this moment in time
in the very final analysis
in the light of present-day developments
an adequate sufficiency
to state quite categorically
personally speaking
strictly off the record
it is our considered opinion that
the overall majority
to focus expressly on the issue that is under review
outstanding performances in the field of athletic endeavour
a violent confrontation situation
the procedure required to secure a satisfactory outcome

2 Make a collection of school jargon – teachers' coinages and textbook terms. Examples: a productive teaching environment = quiet classroom; (from a biology textbook) the process of mastication = chewing.

3 Job titles are often 'jargonised' to make them sound more impressive. Examples:

medical adviser = doctor;
refuse disposal operative = dustman;
law enforcement officer = policeman.

Find other examples and invent titles of your own.

4 Try to explain the meaning of the following piece of official jargon.

Separate departments in the same premises are treated as separate premises for this purpose where separate branches of work which are commonly carried on as separate businesses in separate premises are carried on in separate departments in the same premises.

5 Re-read the passage on page 19 and then try to produce an equally meaningless jargon and cliché-ridden piece of speech for one of the following:

a) A football manager vaguely describing how his team 'got a result'.
b) A scientist failing to clarify a complex chemistry experiment or invention.
c) An art critic's rapturous yet nonsensical review of an exhibition of abstract painting/sculpture.

Words as signposts

The following clusters of words and phrases are 'connectors': words that can be used to knit together the ideas and details in a piece of writing. To a careful reader such words are comprehension cues, signposting the writer's direction. Used sparingly and accurately, they can also aid the fluency of your own writing, particulary when you are handling information and argument.

Addition

and
also
further(more)
in addition
too
again
the following
and then
what is more
moreover
as well as

Summary

in brief/short
on the whole
throughout
in all/overall
to sum up/
    in summary

Announcing opinion/ interpretation

it would seem
one might consider/
    suggest/propose
    suppose/imagine/
    deduce/infer
to conclude

Sequence

initially
first(ly)
then
so far
after(wards)
at last
finally
once
secondly, etc.
next, subsequently
meanwhile
at length
in the end
eventually

Illustration

for example
for instance
such as
as (evidence)
as revealed by
thus
to show that
to take the case of

Restriction

only (if)
unless
except (for)
save for

Emphasis

above all
in particular
notably
specifically
especially
significantly
more important
indeed
in fact

Comparison

equally
similarly
compared with
an equivalent
in the same way
likewise
as with

Persuasion (assuming reader's agreement)

of course
naturally
obviously
clearly
evidently
surely
certainly

Cause and effect

consequently
thus
so
hence
as a result
because/as
therefore
accordingly
since
until
whenever
as long as

Contrast/balance

but
however
nevertheless
alternatively
to turn to
yet
despite this
on the contrary
as for . . .
the opposite
still
instead
on the other hand
whereas
otherwise
although
apart from

Cloze tests

Cloze tests are sometimes called Missing Words Tests and are a useful way of testing the accuracy of your vocabulary. The main benefit is that they supply the context and you have to look for clues in the context in order to come to a thoughtful suggestion: e.g.

Although it was raining, her clothes were quite . . .
Although it was . . ., her clothes were quite dry.

The clues in this sentence are the words 'although' and 'quite'. In the first sentence 'although' suggests that the second part will not refer to the effects of rain and this would lead most people to choose the word 'dry'. In the second sentence 'quite dry' gives you an indication of the amount of wetness in the first part of the sentence. There would therefore be a variety of acceptable alternatives to raining: e.g. snowing.

Another clue in the sentence is the difference between the number in the first part of the sentence and that in the second, i.e. was and were. To do the cloze tests effectively it is also best to read the passage through completely. The run of the passage will then suggest a word immediately; then go back to the beginning and look for the clues contained in the words and grammatical construction. In some of the exercises a pair of words is suggested and you have to pick out the more appropriate one and say how it is more appropriate. In the other passages there are no words suggested. A full stop is indicated by a / sign.

Exercises

1 Both the words in the list of pairs following will fit in the numbered gaps in the passage, but in each case one word is better than the other. Write down which word you would choose and give the reason why you have chosen it in preference to the other word.

a) belief/fear
b) monsoon/rainstorm
c) exaggerated/unreasonable
d) anxiously/long
e) storm/thunder
f) more/less
g) hailstones/raindrops
h) only/scarcely
i) window/pane
j) damaged/smashed
k) theatres/football grounds
l) postponed/cancelled

The _____**a**_____ that haunted many good people that the Crystal Palace would be destroyed by a _____**b**_____ was not so wildly _____ as it now looks. For many of the Londoners who scrutinised the skies so _____**d**_____ on that May morning remembered the extraordinary _____**e**_____ which burst over the city almost five years before, on 1 August 1846. It was on the afternoon of that day that black clouds broke in hail. The storm lasted _____**f**_____ than three hours. The _____**g**_____ were of a monstrous size and did great damage to the city's glass. On the south side there were miles of streets in which _____**h**_____ a single _____**i**_____ of glass was left. Hundreds of skylights were _____**j**_____ and the furnishings of many a poor home were spoiled by the inrushing waters. _____**k**_____ were swamped so badly that performances were _____ .

2 Now complete these cloze exercises:

In _____ Autumn the _____ on the trees are still green. Probably by the end of _____ at least, the green is changing into a _____ brown or red. Because of the _____ of shades of green and the different _____ of colour change, by the middle of October there is a _____ display of different colours. If you look at the trees in a _____ you will see in this display green _____ , _____ , _____ and _____ . By the end of _____ there are not many leaves _____ on the trees. You will see a branch of a tree that has _____ a dozen or so leaves. Suddenly there will be a _____ of wind and _____ leaf will be _____ / _____ to most people the _____ provided by this _____ pattern is beautiful _____ the Local Authority, who have the responsibility for clearing the leaves away when they have _____ , view them _____ .

3 _____ to his parked car, Mr D A Stoddard, of Atlanta, Georgia, discovered the _____ had been stolen and the petrol tank _____ . He went to the garage to buy _____ battery and _____ petrol, and returned to _____ the front _____ wheels missing. He set out _____ , this time to _____ two _____ wheels. He returned to discover _____ the _____ car had vanished. _____ his loss to the police, he was _____ that a policeman, seeing the partly _____ car, had _____ it had been abandoned and made _____ for _____ it away.

4 _____ several weeks had _____ elapsed since he had received the invitation to the wedding, the _____ of _____ to deliver a speech _____ best man still _____ him with _____ .
  Time and _____ _____ he had composed and _____ witty anecdotes, retelling amusing moments he could recall _____ in the company of his _____ friend, only to destroy _____ version, _____ that his words were humourless. _____ the day

finally arrived, he wished that he had never ＿＿＿＿＿ ＿＿＿＿＿ , let
alone been foolish enough to ＿＿＿＿＿ the invitation ＿＿＿＿＿ only
there was ＿＿＿＿＿ ＿＿＿＿＿ who ＿＿＿＿＿ perform the dreaded
chore ＿＿＿＿＿ of him.

5 Read and then rewrite the following passage, choosing the more appropriate word from each of the pairs of alternatives given.

Segovia was a city in a valley of stones – a compact, half-forgotten
(sprawl/heap) of architectural splendours built for the glory of some
(untold/other) time. (Here/Elsewhere) were churches, castles, and medieval walls standing sharp in the evening light, but all dwarfed by that
(extraordinary/unimposing) phenomenon of masonry, the Roman
(viaduct/aqueduct) which (overshadowed/highlighted) the whole. (They/It)
came looping from the hills in a (series/cluster) of arches, (some/one) rising
to over a hundred feet, and composed of blocks of granite weighing several
tons and held (apart/together) by their weight alone. (This/Another) impe-
rial gesture, built to carry water (to/from) a spring ten miles away,
(now/still) strode (around/across) the valley with (massive/delicate) grace, a
hundred vistas (circled/framed) by its (soaring/squat) arches, to
(enter/bypass) the city at last high above the rooftops, (stepping/tip-toeing)
like a mammoth (among/beneath) the houses.

As I Walked Out One Midsummer Morning Laurie Lee

WORDS IN THEIR CONTEXT

Unintended meanings

You must always be aware that words can have more than one meaning and that they can take on unwanted meanings if they are in the wrong company.

Exercises

1 Rewrite the following sentences with the unwanted meaning removed.

   a) A second performance of the play will be given tonight and this will give all those who missed seeing it a further opportunity to do so.

   b) Our picture shows Mr J Smith mowing the lawn with his wife.

   c) As the prisoners passed the iron gate one of them made a bolt for it.

   d) Man assaulted by his wife said to be greatly improved.

   e) When the soup has come to a boil sit on a hot stove and stir frequently.

   f) A well rounded ladies' programme is now being drawn up.

   g) Lord and Lady Smythe received many congratulations after their horse's victory. The latter wore a yellow dress trimmed with chiffon frills.

   h) To open the jar pierce with a pin which releases the vacuum and then push off.

   i) Bishop to Race Greyhounds.

   j) The knitted sock competition resulted in a tie.

2 Make up similar examples of your own, using the above as models.

3 Most of the examples come from newspapers and magazines. Start your own collection of ambiguous statements.

Comprehension

A comprehension passage tests your ability to understand what someone else has written and to express your understanding of it in your own words. In examinations the comprehension question is the great discriminator, that is the marks gained by the candidates range from nought to full; this happens only to a limited extent with the essay or continuous writing. As the comprehension section often counts for up to half of the total marks, success in the examination is nearly always dependent on success in the comprehension section.

Low marks in the comprehension question result from:

1 **careless reading of the passage**
2 **careless reading of the question**
3 **lack of understanding of the passage**
4 **faulty matching of the question with the relevant part of the passage**
5 **inability to express in the candidate's own words ideas from the passage.**

Method of approach

1 Read through the passage quickly without stopping, even if you do not understand parts or individual words.

2 Next, read it through again more slowly, noting:
   a) the build up of ideas or description. It may help you to indicate the sequence of these by numbering them lightly in pencil in the margin or even summarising them in a few words.
   b) the supporting ideas and their relation to the main idea.
      Number these accordingly, e.g. 1(a), 1(b),
   c) illustrations and examples of the ideas,
   d) underline any words which you think are particularly important to the passage.

If you do not understand a word or phrase read through the passage that leads up to it and follows on from it and repeat this two or three times to see if the context gives you a clue. Do not jump to conclusions.

Pay particular attention to the words which indicate the direction of the argument, narrative or description, and make certain you give full value to the function words: e.g. 'We *may* go abroad this summer' is very different from 'We *shall* go abroad this summer'.

3 Read through each question very carefully and, if necessary, underline the important words or phrases: e.g. 'Describe Janet Smith's *attitude* towards school' asks neither for a character description of Janet Smith nor a description of the school.

4 Make certain you obey the instructions in the question: e.g.
Choose 3 of the following 5 phrases.
In your own words describe Janet Smith's appearance.
In not more than 100 words summarise why the author ran away from school.
Quote from the passage the phrase that shows that Janet Smith is moody.

5 If the marks to be awarded for the various questions are indicated, vary the length of your answers accordingly, e.g. if the total marks are 30 and one question is worth 2 marks, then you will probably not need to write more than two or three lines.

6 Sometimes there is such a question as:
How does the writer convey a sense of . . . in the passage?
The following guide should be of help in answering such questions:

a) by choice of words
   i meaning and implication of words, e.g. mob, panic, serene
   ii the sound of the words used, e.g. his cackling laugh changed into a croak
   iii repetition of the same words or words of a similar meaning
b) by use of imagery, e.g. similes and metaphors. Do not say, 'the writer then uses a simile', but show the appropriateness of the comparisons by explaining the points of comparison between the two objects, and what the comparison implies.
c) by descriptive details, e.g. 'As I spoke I saw his knuckles go white'
d) by the actions of the character.

7 When you have written your answer check it once again with the wording of the question.

8 Use the time allowed. While you are composing your answers to the different questions, check frequently that you are keeping to the time allowed.

Marking schemes

Marking schemes should be used with caution. They are relevant only if they relate to:

1 the difficulty of the passage and the questions
2 the time allowed to complete the exercise
3 the overall time allowed for the completion of the examination.

The comprehension exercises which have a marking scheme attached should, therefore, be approached with caution. If any of the above three conditions is varied then the marking scheme can become misleading, and the allocation of the marks may need varying.

Short comprehensions

A Pupil Revolts

Boys sent by their class-masters for punishment by Mr Burgess had to stand in the hall, toeing a white line in front of The Desk. To wait there, facing the grim figure, or even the empty throne, the open chest of canes within sight, was ample torture, especially if the ordeal were prolonged from a
5 quarter to half an hour.

    It broke the nerve of a classmate of mine, when both of us were sent up for persistent talking in school. We had been standing side by side for some time, through a whole session and a playtime, when school was resumed for the last session of the morning and the Head decided to give his attention
10 to us. I saw him rise from his chair, remove his pince-nez, thrust them on their black cord into the breast pocket of his dove-grey waistcoat and replace them by a second pair from the opposite pocket. My legs began to tremble and I felt faintly sick, for the mere act of standing for long always set up the pain and dragging sensation in my back.

15   The Head moved slowly to the chest and began to inspect the canes, a ritual that he performed with theatrical technique. Finally choosing one, and flinging open the Punishment Book, he turned to the row of urchins.

    At that moment the small, inoffensive little boy beside me revolted. He uttered a loud, hysterical cry, dashed to the desk, seized the inkpot and flung
20 it at the awful figure of Majesty. It burst on that dove-grey waistcoat.

For a moment the laws that govern the sun and the stars were suspended. The universe froze into stillness. Then the frantic child flung himself, after the inkpot, against that universe. With another shriek he snatched at the cane in the hand of authority. The Headmaster, towering above him, looked
25 down at this commotion round his feet, while he took out a handkerchief and, with as grave a deliberation as he had changed his pince-nez, dabbed at the ink-stain on the ruined waistcoat. Throwing the handkerchief into the wastepaper basket, he picked up the struggling and impassioned child by the middle of his back and carried him face downwards along the hall, the small
30 limbs making violent motions of swimming in air.

Over the Bridge R Church

Comprehension

1 How do the following add to the overall description of the incident:
   a) The desk? (1)
   b) The sequence of words in the first (2) paragraph suggesting unpleasantness?

2 Quote the word in the first paragraph (2) that sums up how the boys felt at being sent to the Headmaster.

3 What does the phrase 'towering above him' suggest? (2)

4 Explain what is meant by 'The (2) universe froze into stillness'. (line 22)

5 How is the contrast between the size (4) of the Headmaster and that of the boy brought out in the final paragraph? Quote to support your answer.

6 Why do you think the boy acted the (3) way he did?

Total 16

Oral and further written work

7 In pairs, act out an interview between a head-teacher and a fifth-form pupil whom the head is trying to persuade to stay on at school. Tape record the interview and then use this as the basis for:
   a) A play script of the interview (adding necessary stage directions); or
   b) A narrative account of the meeting.

8 Inventing any missing details you might need, write:
   a) the Headmaster's indignant letter to the parents of the boy who threw the inkwell, complaining about the incident; and
   b) the parents' reply.

The Fearless Turk

'So kind,' murmured the Turk, leaving us in some doubt as to whether he was referring to us or himself. There was a pause.

'He's on holiday here,' announced Margo suddenly, as though it was something quite unique.

5 'Really?' said Larry waspishly. 'On holiday? Amazing!'

'I had a holiday once,' said Leslie indistinctly through a mouthful of cake, 'remember it clearly.'

Mother rattled the tea-things nervously, and glared at them.

'Sugar?' she enquired fruitily. 'Sugar in your tea?'

10 'Thank you, yes.'

There was another short silence, during which we all sat and watched Mother pouring out the tea and searching her mind desperately for a topic of conversation. At length the Turk turned to Larry.

'You write, I believe?' he said with complete lack of interest.

15 Larry's eyes glittered. Mother, seeing the danger signs, rushed in quickly before he could reply.

'Yes, yes,' she smiled, 'he writes away, day after day. Always tapping at the typewriter.'

'I always feel that I could write superbly if I tried,' remarked the Turk.

20 'Really?' said Mother. 'Yes, well, it's a gift, I suppose, like so many things.'

'He swims well,' remarked Margo, 'and he goes out terribly far.'

'I have no fear,' said the Turk modestly. 'I am a superb swimmer, so I have no fear. When I ride the horse, I have no fear, for I ride superbly. I 25 can sail the boat magnificently in the typhoon without fear.'

He sipped his tea delicately, regarding our awestruck faces with approval.

'You see,' he went on, in case we had missed the point, 'you see, I am not a fearful man.'

My Family and Other Animals Gerald Durrell

Comprehension

1 In lines 1–9 there are a number of (6) adverbs attached to verbs of saying Select 3 and say what they indicate.

2 In what way is 'modestly' used in line (1) 23?

3 Describe in 2 to 3 lines for each and quote from the passage to support what you say:
   a) Larry's attitude towards the Turk (3)
   b) Margo's attitude towards the Turk (3)
   c) The Mother's attitude towards the (3) situation.

4 a) Why were their faces 'awestruck' (2) (line 26)?
   b) What did the Turk mistake it for? (2)

Total (20)

Castles and Cannons

Until the arrival of gunpowder, well-built castles were virtually impregnable. They consisted of a central, square keep to which the owner could retire should his mercenaries revolt, and which could also be a last-ditch defence should the enemy penetrate the walls. These keeps were surrounded by a
5 deep ditch crossed at the main entrance by a removable drawbridge. The castle often had more than one perimeter wall; these were built tall and thin, and for this reason were called curtain walls. The purpose of high walls was to make them difficult to scale: the longer it took the enemy to climb, the greater the chance of killing him before he reached the top. Height meant
10 protection also against stone-throwing catapults, and against wooden siege engines which attempted to lift men as high as the top of the wall so that they could fight the defenders on their own level. Along the walls ran crenellations (battlements) and machicolations, which were structures jutting out from the wall from which oil and debris could be dropped on the heads
15 of the enemy.

With the arrival of the cannon they were all rendered instantly obsolete. The high curtain walls, so long a secure defence, were easy targets. At the beginning of the fifteenth century various tactics were adopted to protect the castles from the relatively inaccurate bombardment of the early cannon,
20 which hurled piles of stones and rubble. The walls were thickened, sometimes up to fifty feet, and were covered with timber or earth to withstand impact. The crenellations and machicolations were removed, since they were easily knocked off, to fall and crush the defenders behind the walls. Moats were widened so that falling masonry could no longer fill them and form
25 bridges for the attackers. These modifications worked relatively well until developments in metallurgical techniques, coupled with better quality gunpowder, led in the middle of the fifteenth century to the use of more accurate guns which fired iron cannon-balls. The effect of the new guns was devastating, both physically and psychologically. Towns and castles would
30 surrender at the very mention of their arrival.

Connections James Burke

Comprehension

1 Explain two purposes for which the (2)
central keep of a castle proved useful.

2 In your own words, give four reasons (6)
why, before the use of gunpowder,
castle perimeter walls were built 'tall
and thin'.

3 Describe three weaknesses of such (3)
castles against 'the early cannon'.

4 In your own words, describe three (3)
improvements which made later
cannon more effective.

5 Give the meaning of the following
expressions as used in the passage:
a) virtually impregnable (line 1) (1)
b) rendered instantly obsolete (line 16) (2)
c) the effect of the new guns was (3)
devastating, both physically and
psychologically (lines 28–29)

Total (20)

Lake Morning in Autumn

Before sunrise the stork was there
resting the pillow of his body
on stick legs growing from the water.

A flickering gust of pencil-slanted rain
5   swept over the chill autumn morning;
and he, too tired to arrange

his wind-buffeted plumage,
perched swaying a little,
neck-flattened, ruminative,

10   beak on chest, contemplative eye
filmy with star vistas and hollow
black migratory leagues, strangely,

ponderously alone and some weeks
early. The dawn struck and everything,
15   sky, water, birds, reeds

was blood and gold. He sighed.
Stretching his wings he clubbed
the air; slowly, regally, so very tired,

aiming his beak he carefully climbed
20   inclining to his invisible tunnel of sky,
his feet trailing a long, long time.

Douglas Livingstone

Comprehension

1 Using your own words, describe the (3)
stork's stance as accurately as you can.

2 a) We are told in both lines 6 and 18 (4)
that the bird is very tired. Quote 2
other examples from the poem and
show how each one adds to the
impression of the stork's tiredness.
  b) Why exactly is the bird so tired? (1)

3 What do you think the poet means (2)
by saying that the stork is 'strangely,
ponderously alone and some weeks early'?

4 Comment on the author's careful
choice of each of the following words.

Say what you think each word means
and what it seems to suggest.
a) growing (line 3)
b) filmy (line 11)
c) struck (line 14)
d) clubbed (line 17) (4×1)

5 Explain the meaning of the following
phrases as used in the poem:
a) a flickering gust of pencil-
slanted rain (line 4)
b) inclining to his invisible tunnel
of sky (line 20)
c) star vistas and hollow black
migratory leagues (lines 11–12) (3 × 2)

Total (20)

A Kind of Hero

At school he was revered yet lonely.
No other boy, however much
He might dream of it,
Dared to be his friend.
5 He walked, gaunt and piratical,
All bones and grin,
Towards his inescapable end.

Revered, but not by authority,
He poured ink into the new hat
10 Of the French Master,
Painted the blackboard white,
Swore at the huge Principal,
Refused to bend
And invited him to a free fight.

15 In memory he is beautiful,
But only his desperate gold
Hair might have been so.
Vaguely we understood,
And were grateful, that he performed
20 Our lawless deeds:
Punished, he allowed us to be good.

The end: he was killed at Alamein.
He wore handcuffs on the troopship
Going out: his webbing
25 All scrubbed as white as rice;
And we, or others like us,
Were promoted
By his last, derisive sacrifice.

Vernon Scannell

Comprehension

1 Why do you think no other boy dared to be his friend?

2 He is described as 'gaunt and piratical'. In the context of this description what else is hinted at by:
a) He walked . . . towards his inescapable end?
b) All bones and grin?

3 Why did the teachers not revere him?

4 What is there to suggest that the poet realises that he may be glamorising the past?

5 In what way
a) did he perform their lawless deeds?
b) did he allow them to be good?

6 What evidence is there that he was the same as a man as he was as a boy?

7 Explain the last three lines.

The Angry Mountain

Away to the right I caught a glimpse of the front of the lava choking a narrow street and spilling steadily forward. It was black like clinker and as it spilled down along the street, little rivulets of molten rock flowed red.

The air was full of the dust of broken buildings now. My mouth and throat
5   were dry and gritty with it and the air shimmered with intense heat. I could no longer hear the roar of gases escaping from Vesuvius. Instead my world was full of a hissing and sifting – it was a steady, unrelenting background of sound to the intermittent crash of stone and the crumbling roar of falling plaster and masonry.

10   Then the next building began to go. I watched, fascinated, as a crack opened across the roof. There was a tumbling roar of sound, the crack widened, splitting the very stone itself, and then the farther end of the building vanished in a cloud of dust. There was a ghastly pause as the lava consolidated, eating up the pile of rubble below. Then cracks ran splitting
15   all across the remains of the roof not five yards away from me. The cracks widened, spreading like little fast-moving rivers, and then suddenly the whole roof seemed to sink, vanishing away below me in a great rumble of sound and disappearing into the dust of its own fall.

And as the dust settled I found myself staring at the lava face itself. It was
20   a sight that took my breath away. I wanted to cry out, to run from it – but instead I remained on my hands and one knee staring at it, unable to move, speechless, held in the shock of seeing the pitiless force of Nature angered.

I have seen villages and towns bombed and smashed to rubble by shell-fire. But Cassino, Berlin – they were nothing to this. Bombing or shelling
25   at least leaves the torn shells and smashed rubble of buildings to indicate what was once there. The lava left nothing. Of the half of Santo Francisco that it had overrun there was no trace. Before me stretched a black cinder embankment, quite flat and smoking with heat. It was impossible to think of a village ever having existed there. It had left no trace and I could scarcely
30   believe that only a few minutes before there had been buildings between me and the lava and that I'd seen them toppling, buildings that had been occupied for hundreds of years. Only away to the left the dome of a church stood up out of the black plain. And even as I noticed it the beautifully symmetrical dome cracked open like a flower, fell in a cloud of dust and was swal-
35   lowed completely.

The Angry Mountain Hammond Innes

Comprehension

1 Explain what the following mean in
the passage:
   a) intermittent crash of stone (line 9)
   b) pitiless force of Nature (line 22)
   c) the beautifully symmetrical dome
      (line 33)   (3)

2 What pictures do the following images
create in your mind and indicate how
they add to the effectiveness of the
description:
   a) lava choking a narrow street (lines 1–2)
   b) eating up the pile of rubble (line 14)
   c) like little fast-moving rivers (line 16)
   d) cracked open like a flower (line 34)   (8)

3 To which of the senses does the   (8)
description in paragraphs 1–3 appeal?
Give at least 2 supporting references
for each of the senses you name.

4 What made it impossible to think of a   (3)
village having existed there?

Total (22)

Medium length comprehensions

A Strange Job

As summer waned I obtained a strange job. Our next-door neighbour, a
janitor, decided to change his profession and become an insurance agent.
He was handicapped by illiteracy and he offered me the job of accompanying
him on trips into the delta plantation area to write and figure for him, at

5 wages of five dollars a week. I made several trips with Brother Mance, as
he was called, to plantation shacks, sleeping on shuck mattresses,* eating
salt pork and black-eyed peas for breakfast, dinner, and supper; and
drinking, for once, all the milk I wanted.

I had all but forgotten that I had been born on a plantation and I was

10 astonished at the ignorance of the children I met. I had been pitying myself
for not having books to read, and now I saw children who had never read
a book. Their chronic shyness made me seem bold and city-wise; a black
mother would try to lure her brood into the room to shake hands with me
and they would linger at the jamb of the door, peering at me with one eye,

15 giggling hysterically. At night, seated at a crude table, with a kerosene lamp
spluttering at my elbow, I would fill out insurance applications, and a share-
cropper family, fresh from labouring in the fields, would stand and gape.
Brother Mance would pace the floor, extolling my abilities with pen and
paper. Many of the naive black families bought their insurance from us

20 because they felt that they were connecting themselves with something that
would make their children 'write'n speak lak dat pretty boy from Jackson'.

The trips were hard. Riding trains, autos, or buggies, moving from
morning till night, we went from shack to shack, plantation to plantation.
Exhausted, I filled out applications. I saw a bare, bleak pool of black life

25 and I hated it; the people were alike, their homes were alike, and their farms
were alike. On Sundays Brother Mance would go to the nearest country
church and give his sales talk, preaching it in the form of a sermon, clapping
his hands as he did so, spitting on the floor to mark off his paragraphs, and
stomping his feet in the spit to punctuate his sentences, all of which capti-

30 vated the black sharecroppers. After the performance the wall-eyed yokels
would flock to Brother Mance, and I would fill out applications until my
fingers ached.

I returned home with a pocketful of money that melted into the bottom-
less hunger of the household. My mother was proud; even Aunt Addie's

35 hostility melted temporarily. To Granny, I had accomplished a miracle and
some of my sinful qualities evaporated, for she felt that success spelled the

*One made from husks.

reward of righteousness and that failure was the wages of sin. But God called Brother Mance to heaven that winter and, since the insurance company would not accept a minor as an agent, my status reverted to a worldly one;

40   the holy household was still burdened with a wayward boy to whom, in spite of all, sin somehow insisted upon clinging.

Black Boy Richard Wright

Comprehension

1 Show how the author came to obtain his 'strange job' and what exactly he had to do to earn his five dollars a week.   (4)

2 Describe how:
  a) the children, and
  b) the parents of plantation families reacted to the author.   (6)

3 Explain in your own words:
  a) Richard Wright's first feelings about the people he met on the plantations (paragraph 2),and   (3)
  b) why he came to hate what he encountered (paragraph 3).   (2)

4 What makes Brother Mance an effective insurance salesman?   (3)

5 Say what is meant by the following expressions:
  a) bold and city-wise (line 12)
  b) extolling my abilities (line 18)
  c) some of my sinful qualities evaporated (line 36)
  d my status reverted (line 39)   (4 × 2)

6 What happened to the money that the author gained from his job?   (2)

7 In your own words, show how the author's mother, aunt and grandmother reacted differently to his successful return.   (4)

8 How did Richard come to lose his job?   (2)

9 Write Richard's brief account of breakfast in the Wright household on the morning he informed his family that he had lost his job.   (6)

Total (40)

Further written work

10 Write a first-hand account of your own experiences of 'a part-time or holiday job'.

Oral work

11 Discuss the view that early experience of work, such as part-time employment, is just as important as time spent at school.

Hospital Visit

We walked into the ground floor of the hospital, Lydia holding a bunch of mauve tulips which didn't smell even. It was a damn nuisance having to visit Nancy Roberts. It was Lydia who suggested it. 'Nancy would like to see Keith,' she had said. And Keith said awkwardly: 'Course she wouldn't. I'll
5 write if you like.' That was two days ago. We waited for the lift. Somewhere, in this building maybe, a post-mortem was going on. Somewhere upstairs a world of nurses, in antiseptic blue and white, moved carefully from bed to bed. Perhaps a child was being born or maybe right now an intense drama was being enacted in the quiet operating theatre under cold glinting implac-
10 able lights.

Nancy Roberts smiled from ear to ear when she saw us and we sat round her bed awkwardly whilst she admired the tulips.

'You shouldn't have,' she said.

A nurse came by, smiled at us and began putting green screens around
15 the patient next to Nancy. A number of visitors had seated themselves around different beds. The ward had become transformed. The world had come in with presents, flowers, voices. Sunday afternoon. The secret pain lay there, disused for an hour.

In this ward I couldn't smell the antiseptic anaesthetic odour which
20 permeated the Casualty Department that I had noted like a memory when we had entered the hospital. I recognised Mrs Shapiro a few beds away. A nurse said to her, 'Are you comfortable?'

'Thank you, my husband's got five shops,' she replied.

'I like your hat,' said Nancy.
25 'What was it like?' said Keith suddenly. 'The operation . . .?' Nancy smiled. She had been waiting for the question. And she answered with a prepared speech long as a story.

We left the ward solemnly; glad to leave its formality, glad to quit the mansions of the sick and old. Down the whirring lift through the faint ether-
30 odour of the Casualty Department into the street of many colours. Outside the hospital stood a white ambulance. A flower woman stood there smiling, and a student passed us with a stethoscope conspicuously sticking out of his pocket. Keith nearly bumped into a man who stared at the doors of the hospital vacantly, afraid perhaps to go in.
35 We accompanied Lydia home, up the hill, talking and dreaming. Between fragments of conversation I saw myself, self looking upon another self – and that other, a white-gowned, white-masked surgeon. I had recurrent daydreams of myself playing cricket for Glamorgan, scoring the winning goal for Cardiff City, or agitating a responsive crowd, demanding a Government
40 of the People, for the People. But now, looking down at the haggard patient before self's other eyes, I saw that reclining figure assume the familiar features of Nancy Roberts. I said to the beautiful brunette nurse, 'This is inoperable, I will operate.' Only a gasp of amazement and admiration disturbed the silence of the operating room. The anaesthetic bag inflated and

45 collapsed, inflated and collapsed as Nancy Roberts stood on the threshold
of 'Life' and 'Death'.

'We must save the life of Nancy Roberts,' I said to the nurse.

'Impossible,' she answered, 'Even you couldn't do it.' The breathing
continued, diminished; the spectators in the gallery clenched their fists until
50 their knuckles turned white.

'I must try,' I said modestly. 'Now pass me more blood.'

They brought me a bottle of red fluid.

'No,' I said, 'the green blood.'

'Green?' they asked, surprised.

55 'Yes,' I commanded. 'Blood saturated with chlorophyll. It's the only way
to save Nancy Roberts.'

'Where shall we get it?' they queried.

I took a syringe and needle, sticking it into one of my own veins, and the
green corpuscles trickled out, remarkably. When I completed the operation
60 the bladder of air expanded rapidly.

'There you are,' I said. 'Next patient.'

'Don't work any more today,' pleaded a blonde nurse.

'You've been operating twenty-four hours solid, without food, without
water, without sleep.'

65 'I'll take a glass of water,' I remarked. 'The rest can wait. You must not
put self first in a profession like ours.'

'Sir,' said the nurse, 'the next operation is on a man called Keith Thomas –
cancer of the brain.'

'Wheel him in,' I sighed.

70 At the gate of the house we said good-bye to Lydia Pike, and Keith and
I walked down Penylan Hill again.

'You've been very quiet,' said Keith.

'I've been thinking,' I said.

'What?' he asked.

75 'I think I'll become a doctor after all.'

'Thought you were going to be a poet and an assassin,' Keith reminded
me.

'No,' I said. 'One must choose the difficult path. It's too easy to be a poet,
or to knock off a few heads of Europe. Too easy. I'll take the difficult path.
80 Anyway, I believe in Democracy.'

'What'll you be tomorrow?' smiled Keith.

'Dunno,' I said.

Adapted from *Ash on a Young Man's Sleeve* Dannie Abse

Comprehension

1 a) Who were the three people visiting Nancy Roberts?

b) Describe briefly the attitude of each (6) to this visit, as shown in the first paragraph.

2 Pick out from the first paragraph (lines (4) 1–10) 2 groups of words which suggest the impersonal atmosphere of the hospital. Write down under (*a*) and (*b*).

3 Describe in your own words under (*a*) (4) and (*b*) the 2 main changes indicated in lines 16–18) ('The ward had become ... for an hour').

4 What do you think is Nancy's state of (4) mind in lines 25–27 ('Nancy smiled . . . a story')?

5 What contrast does the phrase 'the (4) street of many colours' (line 30) present?

6 What is suggested by the description (2) of the medical student's stethoscope as 'conspicuously sticking out of his pocket' (lines 32–33)?

7 In the last two lines of the passage (81–82), what does the writer suggest
a) about Keith,
b) about himself? (4)

8 'I saw myself, self looking upon (12) another self – and that other, a white-gowned, white-masked surgeon' (lines 36–37). Using quotation, reference and comment, show from lines 40–69 what appeals to the writer in the idea of being a surgeon. You should write about 150 words.

9 Write an account of a real or imagined (10) visit to a person or place, which you have made against your will.

Total (50)

Oxford and Cambridge Board *Paper 1*

A Shock for Emmie

Emmie closed the door softly and stood, listening. From her grandmother's
room came a consoling murmur that told Emmie she was in time. The old
woman slept very little, though she always lay still in her bed all night, bony
nose pointing to the ceiling. She usually got up before anyone else and said
5   her prayers, her thin hands meticulously together and pointing upwards like
long, narrow spearheads. She prayed as if her prayer was a tape-recording
she was sending to a close, beloved relation – a relation who was elderly, like
herself, and rather deaf. Alice, who was embarrassed by her grandmother,
and tried to forestall comment by laughing at her, said that she always ended
10   them, Your Humble and Obedient Servant, Emilia Bean.

Emmie crept downstairs. William, the retriever, did not move when she
went into the kitchen. He lay stiff-legged on the rug, his eyes closed. Only
the plumed tail thumped faintly on the floor. Outside, the ground was still
foggy, but above the mist the sky was delicately blue. Flaxman, the goat,
15   rattled her chain as she lifted her insolent head to stare at Emmie. Emmie
made a face at her and looked at the holly tree. The mother bird perched
on the edge of the nest and fed her gaping changeling; the baby robin lay
dead and unregarded on the ground. Emily pushed it into the bushes with
her foot, so that Alice shouldn't see it, and went out of the garden, along
20   the tow-path towards the houseboats.

On the deck of Riverview, Mrs Hellyer was hanging out washing. She was
an enormous woman with a back like a wall and thick, pale legs. As she bent
over the basket, the hollows at the back of her knees were visible, white as
cold beef fat. She stood up, saw Emmie and called, 'Em, here a minute.'
25   Emmie stopped. 'I've got something for you,' Mrs Hellyer said.

She disappeared inside the boat, and Emmie approached the gangplank
reluctantly. She was fond of Mrs Hellyer, and admired her deeply, but her
affection was tempered by physical distaste. To be hugged, occasionally
kissed, by Mrs Hellyer was a torment; even the sweets she sometimes
30   brought the children had a curious smell as if from long contact with her
heavy, sweating flesh. As Emmie stood on the deck her nostrils quivered.

Mrs Hellyer emerged, wheezing. She held something in her hand. 'Here,'
she said. It was a paper-knife with a carved ivory handle. Emmie looked at
it.

35   'Your Oliver,' Mrs Hellyer said. 'Had it on the tow-path yesterday. Mr
Hellyer gave him half a dollar for it.' She mopped her glistening face with
her apron. 'Kid said he didn't want it but I said to Mr Hellyer, I said it
doesn't do to buy things like that from a child.'

'Oliver shouldn't have taken it. The money,' Emmie said, holding the
40   knife. It was very pretty; the delicately carved handle was cold and smooth
to the touch. She guessed it was valuable. He didn't get this from school,
she thought, appalled.

'He said he picked it up on the rubbish dump but I thought he's found it poking about in the attics, something of the old lady's.'

45 'It's not Gran's,' Emmie looked up, poker-faced. 'I expect he did find it on the rubbish dump. He goes looking for treasure.'

She held her breath. But Mrs Hellyer, usually so well versed in the wickedness of the world, appeared to believe her, 'He oughtn't to go rooting about there, picking up things; you don't know where they've been.'

50 'I'll stop him,' Emmie said. 'And I'll tell him to give back the half-crown.'

'No need,' Mrs Hellyer said kindly. 'I daresay he can do with it, poor little chap.'

The Tortoise by Candlelight Nina Bawden

Comprehension

1 a) What was the 'consoling murmur' (line 2) that Emmie heard?
b) Why was it 'consoling'? (3)

2 Explain the meaning of each of the following phrases as used in the first paragraph:
a) hands meticulously together (line 5);
b) tried to forestall comment by laughing at her (line 9). (2)

3 Explain why Emmie made a face at the goat. (2)

4 What was the 'gaping changeling' (line 17)? (2)

5 Explain the different meanings of the word 'delicately' in the following expressions by substituting another word or a short phrase:
a) delicately blue (line 14);
b) delicately carved (line 40). (2)

6 Name two characteristics that Emmie displays in the first two paragraphs, *before* she meets Mrs Hellyer. (2)

7 Why was Emmie 'appalled' (line 42)? (2)

8 Emmie 'held her breath' (line 47). Explain why. (3)

9 Describe Emmie's contrasting feelings towards Mrs Hellyer, and account for the contradiction in her attitude. (6)

Total (24)

AEB *Paper II*

Examiners' comments

The passage by Nina Bawden proved to be a suitable choice, of about the right level of difficulty, and the statistical analysis of the marks gained on this paper revealed that the questions discriminated well, there being a comparatively wide spread of marks. Naturally, no one gained full marks, as this paper tests not only comprehension, but the additional skills of composing an answer and expressing it accurately.

The most common failing of candidates who scored low marks, apart from the obvious one of inability to understand the extract, once again proved to be casual or careless reading of the passage and questions. Candidates cannot be told too often that the passage needs very close scrutiny. This year the fault manifested itself most plainly in the answers of candidates who failed to understand the interrelationship of the characters in the passage. Thus, despite the evidence in the first two lines, Emmie was confused with her grandmother, Emilia; Emmie was said to hold Alice's attitude towards her grandmother; another character 'Kid', was discovered in line 37; more pardonably, perhaps, Emmie was believed to be Oliver's mother. This last mistake did not affect the marking of any of the answers, although a sensitive reading of the passage would have revealed the true relationship. Another clear example of careless misreading was repeatedly encountered in question 6, when candidates read 'characteristics' as 'characters', somehow interpreted 'displays' to mean 'encounter', and supplied the ridiculous answer 'William and Flaxman'.

A similar fault was the miscopying of words from the passage: names began with small letters, and 'murmer' was written almost as often as the correct form. Other careless errors that were repeatedly penalised were 'forstall', 'coment', 'embarrased', 'gapping', 'changling', 'delicatly', 'appauled' (and all permutations of the '–p's' and '–l's'), 'valuble', 'papper-knife', and 'belive'. Some read line 17 and question 4 so carelessly that they tried to explain 'gaping challenging', and 'delicately *curved*' instead of 'delicately carved' in line 40, question 5.

Almost all the candidates finished the paper, some probably with time to spare as they seemed to have read the passage so carelessly and written such perfunctory answers. However, some weaker candidates compounded their difficulties by answering at inordinate length, occasionally, of course, because they did not in fact know the answer. One wrote twenty-three *lines* explaining 'hands meticulously together' (question 2). He knew the meaning of 'hands' and 'together', and explained these words in some detail, but not of the key word 'meticulously', nor of the phrase as a whole, and so gained no marks. Another wrote forty words explaining 'delicately blue' (question 5); this candidate knew the answer but his expression was repetitive and verbose: 'In the line "but above the mist the sky was delicately blue" it means that it was a pale shade of blue with no clouds, and this could be replaced by "the sky was a light and pure shade of blue".' 'Delicately blue = pale blue' would have earned the mark and expressed the answer more accurately. Answers to question 9 sometimes contained extensive irrelevance, perhaps to while away the time until the examination ended: 'Friends are friends whatever their habits or figure, and Emmie should not have adopted this attitude, she should learn to cope with Mrs Hellyer's faults as a friend', and so on.

Some candidates need instruction in the techniques of answering comprehension questions. It was galling to suspect, or even sometimes to discover, that a candidate knew the answer but had not written it down. This occurred most frequently in the answers to question 7, when candidates wrote vaguely that Emmie was appalled to think where Oliver might have obtained the paper-knife, and then revealed in their answers to question 8 that they realised that she suspected him of stealing it. Some candidates repeated phrases instead of explaining them, on the lines of 'Delicately carved means that the carver had carved the object with a delicate touch'. On the whole, however, transcription was not a serious problem in this paper, as there are few opportunities for candidates to answer questions by simply copying from the paper; this did not deter some candidates from copying out whole sentences in their answers to questions 1, 3, 7, 8 and 9. Some candidates still need to be directed to look at the mark allocated to each question, as an indication of the length of answer required. Some did not realise that a perfunctory answer of two or three lines to question 9 was unlikely to earn six marks.

Finally, the syllabus states that questions may be set on character; therefore there is little excuse for candidates providing evidence of behaviour instead of character traits. For example, the fact that Emmie crept downstairs does not mean that she is necessarily a 'silent' person, as some candidates maintained, but her behaviour in trying to leave the house without attracting her grandmother's attention could well have been used as evidence from which a characteristic could be inferred.

Escape to . . .

Liverpool's missile arrived at the same time as the others. I clung instinctively to the holds as the flash ripped across the sky; a few seconds later the rock trembled slightly and stones clattered down the cliff and fell to the scree below.

5 The echoes died away and we waited. Down in the cwm a sheep called for her lamb and the stream trickled unhurriedly away from the tarn. We waited for a third sense to confirm what two had already told us. We knew and yet waited for confirmation.

The noise was surprisingly gentle. A sound like the banging of a door
10 followed by a prolonged but faraway roaring that welled over the ridge to our left and grew fainter until there was only the stream once more. We could not see over that ridge and we did not want to. My mind emptied completely but my subconscious hung on for what must have been a long time . . . until Peter said quite quietly, 'What shall we do?'

15 I was surprised to find my feet still on the small holds and three fingers still tensed over the vital flake. I looked over my shoulder at Peter belayed on the ledge a few feet below. He was very pale and the rope between us was quite taut. When the flash came he must have thought I would come off: what would it now matter if I had?

20 This was the climb we had dreamt of for a year, our first on Cloggy. And now . . . fierce anger against all the so-called statesmen and their sycophants who had professed to run our world built up inside me and as quickly subsided. There was no point left in that. There was nothing, nothing we could do or say that would be of any use any more. We were here, on our
25 climb, and that was all we had.

I looked again at Peter.

'Up?' I said. He nodded.

It was by far the best climb we had ever done. We were in form, the rocks were dry, the route was varied, difficult and charming. We sat at the top
30 looking down to where the sheep had found her lamb, and coiled up the rope very carefully. We knew we would never need it again. Far to the west the Irish coast sat on the glittering sea, and in front of us Anglesey sprawled green. The east wind sighed gently past, apologetic perhaps for what it was doing.

35 We started up the track above the cliff. We said nothing; we always finished our day by walking to the top of the mountain on whose side we had been climbing. There was no hurry, no hurry at all. We looked appreciatively at the golden sands beyond Caernarvon; I picked up a piece of pink quartz and put it in my pocket. We walked up the track until we reached
40 the railway and the ridge. I looked first, as always before, to the sweeping edge of Crib Gooh, a ridge dear to me for eight years . . . and then to the towering grey haze which was enveloping the whole country, a huge sombre cloud drifting towards us; Arenig had gone, Moel Siabod already was nearly invisible. We watched in silence as the outline of Siabod was blotted out,
45 then turned and walked up the railway to Snowdon's summit.

There were five people already there, standing by the cairn. They said nothing; we did not greet them. We stood and watched. We watched our world die. We stood and prayed and thought of the people and the places and the things . . . there was no bitterness. The haze covered Crib Goch and
50 Lliwedd, and soon a gentle rain of ash began, small grey flakes that settled like a dirty snow. We stood while the sunlight grew dim and our shadows faded away, while the ash pattered finely on the rock and big thunder drops began to fall. We stood until the entire world was fifty yards' radius of rock and scree, a deserted concrete café and a bit of railway . . . the ash settled
55 in our hair and in the folds of our clothes.

I looked at Peter. He smiled.

'I hope Snowdon is climbed again,' he said.

. . . Presently we didn't feel strong enough to stand any longer and sat down . . .

The Climbers' Fireside Book Martyn Berry

Comprehension

1 'We waited for a third sense to confirm what two had already told us.' (lines 6–7)
  a) Name the three senses referred to, and for each one quote a phrase from the passage in evidence. (6)
  b) What did their senses tell them? (2)

2 a) Describe briefly the author's feelings as revealed from line 15 to the end. (6)

b) i Why do you think the author twice mentions a sheep and her lamb (line 5 and line 30)? (3)
   ii Explain fully the meaning of 'apologetic perhaps for what it was doing' (lines 33–34) (3)

3 Imagine that you are a foreign student with little knowledge of Great Britain. What would you learn about Snowdon from reading this passage? (8)

Total (28)

JMB *Paper AII*

For and Against Small Schools

In education, the main theme in rural areas has been reorganisation and consolidation into fewer, larger schools. Primary schools have suffered greatly in this process. In the former East Riding, the number of primary schools dropped from 235 in 1946 to 151 in 1970, a decrease of 36 per cent
5 in twenty-four years. The impetus underlying this movement has been part educational and part economic, with the sceptics laying stress upon the latter. Labour represents a proportionately larger cost in small schools and the minimum 'economic' size is probably a one-form entry school with roughly 210 pupils. Of late, the pace has slackened as the extra costs of
10 transporting children has outstripped the savings made by school closures. There has also been a major report, Gittins on Primary Education in Wales (1967), which proposed a minimum size for primary schools of sixty pupils (say, three teachers) but even this has provoked opposition from defenders of smaller schools. Many schools are still well below the Gittins lower limits
15 and, in practice, it seems that only those with fewer than forty pupils are in danger of 'reorganisation'.

The educational arguments against small rural schools take their cue directly from the modern world. At the upper end of the primary school, the curriculum has expanded so rapidly, to cover subjects such as French,
20 Science, and Music, that there are now too many and diverse interests for one or two teachers to cover adequately, and children in small schools could be disadvantaged by the limited range offered to them. Very similar arguments apply to equipment and materials. Economics apart, it may be physically impossible to house all the equipment considered essential for
25 modern education in a small, out-dated building. Activity spaces, music rooms, television, film projectors and cookery bays, are all extensive in their use of space – which is at a premium in small schools.

The arguments have a psychological and social slant as well. Psychology stresses the dangers inherent in a small school where the dominance of one
30 teacher may be unrelieved; the school could thrive under the influence of a good teacher but equally it may suffer under a mediocre one. Sociology refers to the influx of people from the town into country areas and their demands for urban standards of education which, it is said, are superior and cannot be met within the limitations of a small school.

35 The proponents of the small school are not without arguments of their own to stress. There are advantages derived from small, vertically grouped classes where children of different ages help each other, the older children gaining particularly in terms of responsibility and self-expression. The value of this traditional teaching method has been demonstrated by its adoption
40 in larger, urban schools. Young children also benefit from the confidence and security obtained from smaller groups and from the individual attention allowed by a low pupil–staff ratio and low staff turnover. Discipline is rarely a problem and the vitally important links between home and school can be strong, a point which readily merges with a more general one, namely the

45   social advantages that can be gained by the use of the school as a focal point for community life. With the expanding horizons of the modern world, a demand for a variety of interests could be met by peripatetic teachers serving a group of village schools (and cheaply too; the costs of transporting one person are less than those of transporting an entire school), administrators

50   may prefer smaller units for the flexibility they give in meeting unforeseen population changes and the grouping of children into secondary school catchment areas.

Rural Planning Problems, ed. G E Cherry

Comprehension

1 From the first 3 paragraphs of the passage (lines 1–34) summarise the arguments given in favour of closing down small primary schools in rural areas. Use your own words as far as possible. Your summary should be of some 80–100 words.   (20)

2 In lines 35–46 find 5 different arguments in favour of retaining such schools. Write them down in brief note form, and number them 1 to 5. You may use the words of the original.   (10)

3 From lines 46–52 say briefly what you understand by the italicised words in the following:
a) *peripatetic* teachers   (3)
b) the *flexibility* they give   (3)
c) secondary school *catchment areas*   (4)

Total (40)

Oxford Local *Paper II*

Kibbutzim

A planned attempt to modify family life as we know it has been made in the Jewish organisations in Israel which are called 'kibbutzim'.

They do not repudiate the idea that a father is responsible for his family but they do arrange for him to have a less intense relationship with his chil-
5   dren; he spends a happy hour or two with them each day and longer at the weekend, but he is not responsible for discipline, nor for the regulation of their lives.

Most kibbutzim represent some form of agricultural village in which all property and products are communally owned, and living, including the
10   rearing of children, is organised on a collective basis. The kibbutzim were founded on the idea that physical labour is honourable and an end in itself. A distinction is made between productive labour and work which merely provides services for the community, such as cooking, laundering or bringing up small children. These latter jobs carry lower status because they are
15   'unproductive'.

Within the original kibbutzim the family was not expected to survive because the stress was upon the individual and upon the community, with

20 no recognised intermediate groups. Three principles on which the kibbutzim were founded were resistance to the authoritarian figure of the father, the raising of the status of women and the lessening of children's dependence on the family.

Children who are brought up in the Infant House from the age of four days, and then in the Toddlers' House and boarding school, do not feel dependent on their fathers legally or economically, and the father certainly
25 has no authoritarian position. There is no 'master of the household', nor do parents have the physical care and upbringing of their children. None of the traditional characteristics of the family survive in the kibbutzim, but it is interesting to find that a strong psychological bond continues. Parents and children are deeply attached to each other and spend as much time together
30 as they possibly can. Some parents work through the heat of the day and take no siesta so that they can be with their children when they finish school. When a child is brought up day and night with his fellows his parents are the only area of his life that he does not have to share, so his moments with them are very precious. It may be that the father is especially valued because
35 all the nurses and the teachers in primary school are women.

Since most of the daily care of the children is done by the 'metapelets' or nurses, the time they spend with their parents is regarded as a free or leisure period. In some ways the parents in the kibbutzim occupy almost the same position as grandparents in most Western societies, and the mothers and
40 children do not have the bond of having gone through periods of stress and strain together.

Reverence for the old works in reverse in the kibbutzim. Children are graded in school strictly according to age but as soon as they join the community they are supposed to have complete equality with all adults. The
45 highest honour goes to the most efficient worker, which means that the middle-aged man who cannot do as much as he did feels inferior. The young are more valuable because of their better economic earning pwer. As soon as the children's working powers mature they compete with their parents and they generally win because they are stronger.

Comprehension

In answering the following questions you are asked to use your own words as far as possible, to keep within the required number of words, and to use only information that is contained in the passage.

1 What part is a father *expected* to play (5) in the lives of his children in the kibbutzim? (Use no more than 50 words.)

2 Describe what in practice the (10) children's relationships are with their parents during their upbringing. (Use between 70 and 90 words.)

3 What attitudes to work in the (5) kibbutzim are revealed? (50 words should be sufficient.)

Total (20)

Welsh Joint Education Committee

An Interesting Character

Canon Rawnsley had been vicar of Wray, a parish on Lake Windermere, when Beatrix was twelve years old, and not many years after this Mr Potter had discovered Wray Castle, an example of the Victorian baronial style, appropriately furnished and very much to his taste, which could be rented
5   in the summer. He added it to the list of large houses, both in Scotland and the Lakes, which he occupied according to choice in the holiday months, and it was from here that Beatrix, in the years of growing up and in her twenties, came to know the lakes and fells, the scattered farms and lonely places of this poetic and beautiful part of the north country.

10   She and her parents also, in the course of their Wray Castle summers, came to know Canon Rawnsley; the acquaintance survived the Canon's removing from Wray to become vicar of Crosthwaite, near Keswick, and both Beatrix and her family delighted, for different reasons, in the invigorating company of this most charming of men. Mr Potter found him inter-
15   esting as an authority on the Lake Country, with already a number of published books to his credit; he was moreover ready to give advice on Mr Potter's new hobby of collecting autographed letters of the Lake Poets, and to correspond with him freely on religious matters in a brisk and uninhibited style which, since there were very few people who could decipher the
20   Canon's handwriting, provided almost a sporting interest for Mr Potter. To Beatrix he was even more appealing, for in the warmth of his physical and mental vigour, which was prodigious, her shyness melted, and she made the stimulating discovery that it was possible for grown-up people to have enthusiasms.

25   The Canon had many, and was always ready to give battle or bully a committee on behalf of any of them. He had become by common consent the champion of the Lakes, challenging and defying the builders of bungalows and the extenders of railways, tilting single-handed against all the dangers which already menaced this lovely and tripper-ridden district.

30   When the Potters first encountered him he was crusading hotly for the formation of a National Trust to buy and preserve places of natural beauty and historic interest for the nation – an ambition which he achieved in 1895, together with Miss Octavia Hill and Sir Robert Hunter. These three working together were an ideal combination for the purpose. Octavia Hill, well
35   known as a sincere philanthropist, was the right figure to engage public sympathy; Sir Robert Hunter gave legal knowledge and his natural ingenuity to the cause; Canon Rawnsley was the dynamo. From the foundation of the Trust, the Canon became more than ever jovially formidable in the north. He waged war on jerry-builders, like a scorpion he skirmished round the
40   demolishers of ancient bridges, he spiked the guns of expanding tramway companies. He was prepared to travel anywhere and tackle anybody, and the ring of his energetic boots and the very shadow of his beard struck terror into council meetings and committees.

All this was very interesting to Beatrix, who sympathised with his views
45   and admired his pugnacity, and the Canon had other endearing qualities

which drew her to him. He was an amateur naturalist, like herself, and in his boyhood skinned and stuffed and anatomised to the very limits of endurance. He was an antiquarian, too, as well as a lover of nature, and liked nothing better than to raise a fund to erect a stone to commemorate some-
50 thing or somebody that everyone else had forgotten; unless, perhaps, it were to walk his friends all night over the fells to reach a particular peak in time for a special sunrise, which he would contemplate with a picnic basket and describe afterwards in a sonnet. He wrote verses on any and every occasion, sometimes in a vein of romping rectory humour, and always without the least
55 shadow of self-consciousness. He published his verses in book form and sent them to the newspapers, without misgiving as without pretentiousness, always regarding them (as indeed they were) simply as an agreeable way of saying this or that, and an innocent diversion. One cannot complete the catalogue of his achievements and activities without adding that he was an
60 ardent traveller, the author of more than a score of books, a Canon of Carlisle, a friend of Tennyson, a campaigner against objectionable postcards and a great organiser of bonfires. It is worth mentioning that on the night of Queen Victoria's Jubilee in 1887 no fewer than 148 of Canon Rawnsley's bonfires could be seen from the top of Skiddaw.
65 This lively and engaging clergyman was the first man of letters, the first published author whom Beatrix had encountered; he had taken a great interest in her funguses and had encouraged her painting (even those fantasies which she invented for children at Christmas, and which her elderly aunts at Putney considered 'silly'); so that it was to him that she naturally
70 turned for advice when the idea occurred to her, as it did in her middle thirties, that she might privately venture on a modest little children's book, 'The Tale of Peter Rabbit'.

One Tale of Beatrix Potter Margaret Lane

Comprehension

1 Give the meaning of these expressions as they are used in the passage:
   a) appropriately furnished (line 4)
   b) the acquaintance survived the Canon's removing (lines 11–12)
   c) invigorating company (lines 13–14)
   d) by common consent (line 26)
   e) sincere philanthropist (line 35)
   f) admired his pugnacity (line 45)
   g) endearing qualities (line 45)   (15)

2 For what reasons did (i) Mr Potter   (12)
   and (ii) Beatrix find Canon Rawnsley interesting?

3 What do you learn from the passage   (15)
   about the enthusiasms of Canon Rawnsley and the various things he did in pursuit of these enthusiasms? Answer in about 100 of your own words.

4 What different abilities did the three   (6)
   founders of the National Trust contribute? Answer in your own words.

5 Write 2 short sentences in your own   (4)
   words, one about the nature of Canon Rawnsley's poetry and the other about the Canon's attitude to his own poetry.

Total (52)

JMB *Paper C*

Examiners' comments

The passage, taken from Margaret Lane's biography of Beatrix Potter, was competently, if at times carelessly, read by most candidates. Surprisingly, most candidates assumed that 'Canon' was a Christian name.

The vocabulary question was fairly well done, but few understood the meaning of 'philanthropist' or 'pugnacity'. As usual, care and precision were rewarded while casual approximations scored low marks.

Most candidates were able to cope at least adequately with question 2, except that there was widespread difficulty in interpreting the phrase 'authority on the Lake District'; some answers suggested that Canon Rawnsley held some sort of official position.

A noticeable feature of responses to 3, obviously a major question, was that many candidates seemed to prefer their own question to the one on the question paper. Thus, there were lengthy paragraphs on the *character* of Rawnsley, with only incidental reference to the key points of his enthusiasms and actions in pursuit of them. Those who did write relevantly sometimes lost marks by relying on distinctive phrases from the passage, such as 'waged war on jerry-builders', 'crusading hotly' and 'skinned and stuffed and anatomised to the very limits of endurance'.

It was rare to find good answers to questions 4 or 5, where again there was too much copying from the passage, despite the clear instructions in these two questions.

Comparison of passages – varying lengths

Women and Fashion

The two extracts that follow are from a book discussing the development of women's fashion in the nineteenth century and the way this development was connected with the growing Women's Rights movement. In passage A 'active' refers to being active in the movement, as was Millicent Fawcett.

Passage A

Portraits, drawings, engravings, and even photographs of the women who were most active in the late 1860s have survived. From their looks and their dress it seems that good sense and moderation guided their taste. It is difficult to find any outward trace of the masculine woman dreaded (or
5 hoped for as a target) by opponents of their enfranchisement. In the National Portrait Gallery is a touching painting by Ford Madox Brown of Henry Fawcett and his wife Millicent. Her golden-red hair, of the colour so much admired by the Pre-Raphaelites (i.e. the painters and artists of that time), is dressed in the fashion of the moment and she sits perched on the
10 arm of her husband's chair, her arm round his shoulders, her dark grey dress livened by a splash of colour as it is caught up, apparently by accident, so that her red crinolined underskirt shows.

Passage B

If the Opposition's vision of the strong-minded woman is difficult to discover as a historic personage, the disapproving newspaper reports are consistent in their description of her appearance, and these are confirmed by illustrations to jokes at her expense in *Punch*. In these her hair is usually
5 cut short to the nape of her neck (it varies a little in its actual length) and her dress is dark, severe and often includes the kind of square-cut jacket that was obviously appropriate to the country gentry but wrong in town.

It is natural that women with lively and fully occupied minds should have found it irksome to conform rigidly to the fashions in dress worn by the
10 majority of conventional women. Even the constant changes of fashion itself seemed to symbolise infirmity of purpose to those whose ambition it was to appear sufficiently stable and reliable to be entrusted with the Vote, but since fashion is invincible, those who tried to escape it in their dress found themselves and their ideas caught up and swept along as a part of its stream.

Health Art and Reason, Stella M Newton

Comprehension

Passage A

1 Give the meaning of the following
as used in the passage:
a) enfranchisement (line 5)
b) good sense and moderation
guided their taste (line 3)   (2 × 2)

2 What is implied by the statement   (2)
in brackets *or hoped for as a target*?

3 The pose for the painting was   (3)
obviously very carefully thought
out. What do you think it was
meant to suggest?

Passage B

4 Explain what the following mean
as used in the passage:
a) historic personage (line 2)
b) appropriate to the country
gentry (line 7)
c) conventional women (line 10)
d) irksome (line 9)
e) infirmity of purpose (line 11)
(In addition, try to find out the
origin of the phrase. A Dictionary
of Quotations will help.)
f) fashion is invincible (line 13)   (6 × 2)

5 Do you agree that:
a) women with lively and fully
occupied minds find it irksome
to conform to fashion?
b) fashion is invincible?
Give reasons for your answers.   (2 × 3)

Both passages

6 Which phrase in B seems to repeat   (1)
the phrase *masculine woman* in A?

7 What is the connection between   (3)
the description of the painting of
Millicent and the statement in the
first two lines of B, 'If the . . .
personage'?

8 Using 2 separate columns,   (6)
compare detail by detail the
painting by Ford Madox Brown
and the cartoons of women in
Punch.

9 How do these two passages show   (3)
that even evidence from the time
is not always reliable when we
make judgements about the past?

Total (40)

The Hunters in the Snow

The over-all picture is winter
icy mountains
in the background the return

from the hunt it is toward evening
5   from the left
sturdy hunters lead in

their pack the inn-sign
hanging from a
broken hinge is a stag a crucifix

10 between his antlers the cold
inn yard is
deserted but for a huge bonfire

that flares wind-driven tended by
women who cluster
15 about it to the right beyond

the hill is a pattern of skaters
Brueghel the painter
concerned with it all has chosen

a winter-struck bush for his
20 foreground to
complete the picture.

William Carlos Williams

1 The drawing
What impression do you get from the manner
in which the hunters and dogs are walking?
How do they contrast with the skaters?

2 The poem
What is the effect of leaving out the
punctuation marks? Give 2 examples of the
way the meaning is changed according to
where you pause.

3 Which words or phrases suggest the coldness
of the snow?

4 Pick out a detail which is prominent in the
poem but not so prominent in the drawing.
What is the effect of this change of
emphasis?

Spring and Fall: To a Young Child

Margaret, are you grieving
Over Goldengrove unleaving?
Leaves, like the things of man, you
With your fresh thoughts care for, can you?
5   Ah! as the heart grows older
It will come to such sights colder
By and by, nor spare a sigh
Though worlds of wanwood leafmeal lie;
And yet you *will* weep and know why.
10   Now no matter, child, the name:
Sorrow's springs are the same.
Nor mouth had, no nor mind, expressed
What heart heard of, ghost guessed:
It is the blight man was born for,
15   It is Margaret you mourn for.

Gerard Manley Hopkins

First Frost

A girl is freezing in a telephone booth,
huddled in her flimsy coat,
and face stained by tears
and smeared with lipstick.

5   She breathes on her thin little fingers.
Fingers like ice. Glass beads in her ears.

She has to beat her way back alone
down the icy street.

First frost. A beginning of losses.
10   The first frost of telephone phrases.

It is the start of winter glittering on her cheek,
the first frost of having been hurt.

Andrei Voznesensky

Comprehension

1 These two poems are similar in that the girls in both are being introduced to the sadness and unhappiness that exist in life.
   a) In what way do they differ?
   b) Would both poems be as effective if they were about boys?

Spring and Fall

2 What is the stated reason for Margaret's weeping? What does the poet say is the real reason?

3 What, according to Hopkins, will happen to the girl as she grows older?

4 What do lines 9–12 mean?

5 What does the last line mean?

6 The poem contains a number of words made up by the poet, e.g. wanwood from wan and wood, with associations of wormwood; leaf-meal has associations of piecemeal. What does the poem gain from this? What does the name, Goldengrove, suggest?

7 Explore all the implications of the title, *Spring and Fall*.

First Frost

8 What is the feeling in the first four lines? Pick out the words which help to create that feeling.

9 How does the poet suggest the girl's vulnerability and loneliness?

10 What do you think she had just been told on the telephone? Can you justify your answer?

11 Explain what the terms 'First Frost', 'A beginning of losses' and line 11 mean. For the latter, pay particular attention to the word 'glittering'.

12 In both poems, the moods described are in harmony with the time of year:
   a) describe moods of your own which were in harmony with the seasons
   b) describe occasions when the world within you was at complete variance from the world outside you.

How to Survive

In passage A, Pizarro is the leader of the Spaniards who invaded and conquered Peru in the sixteenth century.

In passage B the conversation takes place shortly after a war in Eastern Europe in the last century. The invading army has been defeated. The Man, who is obviously an officer from the defeated army, breaks into the room of Raina, the daughter of a local wealthy business man, and forces her to hide him when the soldiers search the house for him. The soldiers leave satisfied that no one is hiding there.

Passage A

YOUNG MARTIN   What is it, sir?

PIZARRO   A wound from long ago. A knife to the bone. A savage put it into me for life. It troubles me at times . . . You'll start long before me with your wounds. With your killing too. I wonder how you'll like that.

5 YOUNG MARTIN   You watch me, sir.

PIZARRO   I will. You deal in deaths when you are a soldier, and all your study should be to make them clean, what scratches kill and how to cut them.

YOUNG MARTIN   But surely, sir, there's more to soldiering than that?

10 PIZARRO   You mean, honour, glory – traditions of the service?

YOUNG MARTIN   Yes, sir.

PIZARRO   Dungballs. Soldiers are for killing: that's their reason.

YOUNG MARTIN   But, sir –

PIZARRO   What?

15 YOUNG MARTIN   It's not just killing.

PIZARRO   Look, boy: know something. Men cannot just stand as men in this world. It's too big for them and they grow scared. So they build themselves shelters against the bigness, do you see? They call the shelters Court, Army, Church. They're useful against loneliness, Martin, but

20 they're not true. They're not real, Martin. Do you see?

YOUNG MARTIN   No, sir. Not truthfully sir, . . .

PIZARRO   No, sir. Not truthfully sir! Why must you be so young? Look at you. Only a quarter formed. A colt the world will break for its sightless track. Listen once. Army loyalty is blasphemy. The world of soldiers is

25 a yard of ungrowable children. They play with ribbons and make up ceremonies just to keep out the rest of the world. They add up the number of their blue dead and their green dead and call that their history. But all this is just the flower the bandit carves on his knife before shoving it into a man's side . . . What's Army Tradition? Nothing but years of Us against

30 Them. Christ-men against Pagan-men. Men against men. I've had a life of it boy, and let me tell you it's nothing but a nightmare game, played by brutes to give themselves a reason.

YOUNG MARTIN   But sir, a noble reason can make a fight glorious.

PIZARRO   Give me a reason that stays noble once you start hacking off

35 limbs in its name. There isn't a cause in the world to set against this pain. Noble's a word. Leave it for the books.

YOUNG MARTIN   I can't believe that, sir.

PIZARRO   Look at you – hope, lovely hope, it's on you like dew. Do you know where you're going? Into the forest. A hundred miles of dark and

40 screaming. The dark we all came out of, hot. Things flying, fleeing, falling dead – and their death unnoticed. Take your noble reasons there, Martin. Pitch your silk flags in that black and wave your crosses at the wild cats. See what awe they command. Be advised, boy. Go back to Spain.

YOUNG MARTIN   No, sir. I'm coming with you. I can learn, sir.

45 PIZARRO   You will be taught. Not by me. The forest.

He stumps out.

The Royal Hunt of the Sun Peter Shaffer

Passage B   *Raina walks with studied elegance to the ottoman and sits down. Unfortunately she sits on the pistol, and jumps up with a shriek. The man, all nerves, shies like a frightened horse to the other side of the room.*

THE MAN (*irritably*)   Don't frighten me like that. What is it?

RAINA   Your revolver! It was staring that officer in the face all the time. What an escape!

THE MAN (*vexed at being unnecessarily terrified*)   Oh, is that all?

5   RAINA (*staring at him rather superciliously as she conceives a poorer and poorer opinion of him, and feels proportionately more and more at her ease*)   I am sorry I frightened you. (*She takes up the pistol and hands it to him.*) Pray take it to protect yourself against me.

THE MAN (*grinning wearily at the sarcasm as he takes the pistol*)   No use,
10   dear young lady: there's nothing in it. It's not loaded. (*He makes a grimace at it, and drops it disparagingly into his revolver case.*)

RAINA   Load it by all means.

THE MAN   I've no ammunition. What use are cartridges in battle? I always carry chocolate instead; and I finished the last cake of that hours ago.

15   RAINA (*outraged in her most cherished ideals of manhood*)   Chocolate! Do you stuff your pockets with sweets – like a schoolboy – even in the field?

THE MAN (*grinning*)   Yes: isn't it contemptible? (*Hungrily*) I wish I had some now.

RAINA   Allow me. (*She sails away scornfully to the chest of drawers. and
20   returns with the box of confectionery in her hand.*) I am sorry I have eaten them all except these. (*She offers him the box.*)

THE MAN (*ravenously*)   You're an angel! (*He gobbles the contents.*) Creams! Delicious! (*He looks anxiously to see whether there are any more. There are none: he can only scrape the box with his fingers and suck them.
25   When that nourishment is exhausted he accepts the inevitable with pathetic good humour, and says, with grateful emotion*) Bless you, dear lady! You can always tell an old soldier by the inside of his holsters and cartridge boxes. The young ones carry pistols and cartridges: the old ones, grub. Thank you. (*He hands back the box. She snatches it contemptuously from
30   him and throws it away. He shies again, as if she had meant to strike him.*) Ugh! Don't do things so suddenly, gracious lady. It's mean to revenge yourself because I frightened you just now.

RAINA (*loftily*)   Frighten me! Do you know, sir, that though I am only a woman, I think I am at heart as brave as you.

35   THE MAN   I should think so. You havent been under fire for three days as I have. I can stand two days without showing it much; but no man can stand three days: I'm as nervous as a mouse. (*He sits down on the ottoman, and takes his head in his hands.*) Would you like to see me cry?

RAINA (*alarmed*)   No.

40   THE MAN   If you would, all you have to do is to scold me just as if I were a little boy and you my nurse. If I were in camp now, they'd play all sorts of tricks on me.

RAINA (*a little moved*)   I'm sorry. I won't scold you. (*Touched by the*

45 *sympathy in her tone, he raises his head and looks gratefully at her: she*
immediately draws back and says stiffly) You must excuse me: our soldiers
are not like that. (*She moves away from the ottoman.*)

THE MAN   Oh yes they are. There are only two sorts of soldiers: old ones
and young ones. I've served fourteen years: half of your fellows never
50 smelt powder before. Why, how is it that you've just beaten us? Sheer
ignorance of the art of war, nothing else . . .

Arms and the Man Bernard Shaw

Comprehension

Passage A

1 Point out the contrast between the attitudes
of Martin and Pizarro to killing and support
with references.

2 What does Pizarro mean when he says
   a) 'Men cannot just stand as men in this
      world.' (lines 16–17)?
   b) 'Do you know where you're going? Into
      the forest. A hundred miles of dark and
      screaming.' (lines 38–40)?

3 According to Pizarro what purpose do the
Court, Army and Church serve?

4 Say which of the following describe Pizarro
and give reasons for your answer:
   a) happy
   b) optimistic
   c) lonely
   d) cynical
   e) realistic
   f) cruel

Passage B

5 What do the stage directions tell us about the
two people?

6 Which of their words and actions support
what the stage directions tell us?

7 How do their attitudes towards heroism and
war differ?

Both passages

8 Give point by point the ways in which the two
extracts:
   a) resemble each other;
   b) differ from each other.

Further topics to consider

9 a) How significant is it in the two plays that
      it is the young people who have romantic
      views of war, whereas the older ones
      dislike it?
   b) Do you think this still applies?

10 a) Do you think that war can ever be a way
       for satisfying any people's desire for
       adventure, action and heroism?
    b) If you think it cannot, how do you think
       it can be satisfied?

Dining on the Trans-Siberian Express

Passage A

The dining-car was certainly unchanged. On each table there still cer-
emoniously stood two opulent black bottles of some unthinkable wine, false
pledges of conviviality. They were never opened, and rarely dusted. They
may contain ink, they may contain the elixir of life. I do not know. I doubt
5 if anyone does.

Lavish but faded paper frills still clustered coyly round the pots of paper
flowers, from whose sad petals the dust of two continents perpetually threatened the specific gravity of the soup. The lengthy and trilingual menu had
not been revised; 75 per cent of the dishes were still apocryphal,* all the
10 prices were exorbitant. The cruet, as before, was of interest rather to the
geologist than to the gourmet. Coal dust from the Donetz Basin, tiny flakes
of granite from the Urals, sand whipped by the wind all the way from the
Gobi Desert – what a fascinating story that salt-cellar could have told under
the microscope! Nor was there anything different about the attendants. They
15 still sat in huddled cabal at the far end of the car, conversing in low and
disillusioned tones, while the 'chef du train', a potent gnome-like man,
played on his abacus a slow significant tattoo. Their surliness went no deeper
than the grime upon their faces; they were always ready to be amused by
one's struggles with the language or the cooking. Sign-language they inter-
20 preted with more eagerness than apprehension: as when my desire for a
hard-boiled egg – no easy request, when you come to think of it, to make
in pantomime – was fulfilled, three-quarters of an hour after it had been
expressed, by the appearance of a whole roast fowl.

One's Company Peter Fleming

* doubtfully authentic/sham.

Passage B

Next there is the matter of food, the other great event of the day. You
can with success visit the restaurant of Rossiya – if you have a telepathic
sense of timing – and the journey will take you across a devil's leap: the
barely insulated connecting platform between the cars where you cling to
5 frosty rails at the point of the train's greatest mechanical turbulence; the cold
wind shouts, and the blast reminds you of the real scale of what is being done
here. The rapidshooter's reward is a Tsarist salon in dark polished wood and
cream of the kind presumed to be left behind on the Nakhoda sleeper,
operated by motherly 'mujiks' swathed from head to foot in what look like
10 single great sweatrags. They tot on an abacus governed by an impenetrable
system, and work from a twelve-page menu printed in four languages which
boasts every conceivable national delicacy from 'blinis' to red currant vodka;
a point which should by no means distract you from the fact that the choice
is always limited to beefsteak and cheese. However, you are not allowed to

15 order until you have studied the menu attentively. Actually to be fair, this
is to ignore the excellent black bread, robust and tangy, the rich jam and
the excellent tea. Chekov, implacable in these matters, found Siberian tea
to have the flavour of sage and beetles, but I find it sweet and light. Delicious. Also, there is suspicious milk and gallons of bottled plums and sherry-
20 type wine; and comfortable meat and vegetable soups crop up more often
now that the whole new consignment of provisions taken on at Irkutsk is
seen to repair the ravages on the system of not only feeding the travellers
for some days but also of acting as local grocery store to forty-odd towns
on the way. There is also the occasional blast of canned peas that arrives
25 on the plate frozen as the landscape of Siberia, reminding you of how much
worse it could be.

Rossiya Michael Pennington

Comprehension

Passage A

1 Find three items of evidence which (2)
suggest that the author has travelled
on the Trans-Siberian Express before.

2 Why does Peter Fleming remark that (2)
the cruet 'was of interest rather to
the geologist than to the gourmet'?

3 Describe in your own words your (3)
impression of the attendants who
served in the dining car. Show how
their initial appearance was somewhat
misleading.

Passage B

4 Why exactly did a visit to the dining (2)
car involve 'a telepathic sense of
timing and a degree of danger'?

5 Show how the provisions taken on at (2)
Irkutsk were beneficial in two senses.

6 Summarise Michael Pennington's (3)
attitude to the food offered on the
train. (50 words approximately)

Both passages

7 Explain the meaning of:
a) perpetually threatened the specific
gravity of the soup (A, lines 7–8)
b) pantomime (A, line 22)
c) the rapidshooter's reward (B, line 7)
d) every conceivable national delicacy (8)
(B, line 12)

8 How do both writers, for all their (4)
attention to the dining-car, still stress
the sheer scope of the Trans-Siberian
journey?

9 What similarities and differences do
you find in the two writers'
recollections of:
a) the menu
b) the activities of the dining-car (4)
attendants?

10 How do the two accounts differ (4)
despite their similarity of subject?

11 Imagine that you are a visitor from (6)
abroad travelling on a British train
for the first time. Produce 15 lines
from an account of the journey,
describing your experiences in the
dining-car. (Humorous imitation of either
of the two passages might prove effective.)

Total (40)

Multiple choice – varying lengths

For the following comprehensions, select one of the four alternative answers for each question. The possible alternatives for the first comprehension are discussed in detail under 'Comments on the answers'.

Winter Scene

Dutch artists of the seventeenth century did not aim at grand and elevated effects, as did the Italians at this period. Holland was a republic, and artistic patronage was not dominated by the aristocratic taste for magnificence. The Dutch painted ordinary things, and their pictures appealed to ordinary
5 people. They were cheap enough for the middle classes to afford, and they were seen also in humbler places such as the shops of butchers, bakers and cobblers, or in the houses of common farmers, which were full of pictures, according to the diarist John Evelyn. The most popular subjects reflected the Dutch scene, in this case the canals, which froze over every winter.
10 The earliest winter landscapes formed part of medieval series of the occupations of the months, or were backgrounds to religious scenes. But by

the seventeenth century, landscapes were painted for their own sake; van
Goyen was a specialist in landscape. He was born in Leiden, though eventually he settled in The Hague, where he was a respected member of the
15   Artists' Guild and was commissioned by the Municipality to paint a pan-
oramic view for the Burgomaster's room. On the other hand, van Goyen was
constantly travelling, and often in financial trouble. He died insolvent,
having speculated in land and tulips, as well as in art dealing. His landscapes
perhaps reflect something of his character in their freedom and in their
20   feeling for the changing and insubstantial qualities of light.

    Winter scenes painted early in the century presented a pageant of tiny,
colourfully dressed and detailed figures scattered over the pale ice. This was
the manner in which Jan van Goyen worked originally, but in the 1620s the
fashion changed. Dutch artists depicted landscape in a different manner,
25   bringing out the overall atmosphere rather than the details, and subordi-
nating the different colours to an almost monochromatic colour scheme.
Compositions too became less diffuse and more unified, dominated by large
areas of sky and cloud, and low flat horizons.

    In this *Winter Scene*, van Goyen has achieved the particular effect of a
30   dull winter afternoon, with a very freely painted technique and a colour
scheme restricted mainly to browns and greys. The wintry light, painted in
a very pale cream colour, breaks through the grey clouds in the centre, and
its reflections glint in the ice beneath the huddled figures. This light enlivens
the whole scene, as though the weather has suddenly brightened. The effect
35   of veiled, shifting cloud is conveyed by using very thin paint, letting the
prepared ground of the wood panel shine through the greyish brushstrokes,
and a sense of space is given by the patches of pale blue sky and tiny birds.
The trees at the right are delicately painted, the paint trailed almost casually
on to the surface, and throughout one can follow the movement of the
40   artist's brushes.

    This spontaneity, which contrasts with the concern for minute finish shown
by the Dutch still life and interior painters, comes only from long experience. Van Goyen was a very prolific artist, and made hundreds of drawings
from nature in a vivid and rapidly executed style which must have had an
45   effect on the way he handled a brush.

Twenty Paintings J Treuherz

Multiple choice comprehension

1 The subject of Van Goyen's painting, according to the passage, is
   a) flooded meadows which have iced over
   b) winter occupations in Holland
   c) a bright winter morning
   d) a frozen canal scene

2 The author suggests in the first paragraph that seventeenth-century Dutch art was
   a) grandiose and pompous
   b) not similar to Italian art of the time
   c) controlled by the wishes of the aristocracy
   d) bought only by wealthy patrons

3 All of the following ideas are brought out in the first paragraph *except*
   a) Dutch painting at the time was not expensive to buy
   b) landscape subjects were not often painted
   c) everyday scenes were often the subjects of paintings
   d) it wasn't only the rich who owned paintings

4 Paragraph 2 is *chiefly* concerned with
   a) the history of landscape painting
   b) van Goyen's career as a landscape artist
   c) van Goyen's life style
   d) van Goyen's reputation as an artist

5 The semi-colon in line 12
   a) indicates that what follows still refers to landscape painting
   b) could as conveniently have been a comma
   c) makes too big a break in the meaning
   d) shows the list that follows to be important

6 'insolvent' (line 17) is most accurately replaced by
   a) wealthy
   b) bankrupt
   c) disgraced
   d) poor

7 The expression 'the manner in which Jan van Goyen worked originally' (lines 23) refers to
   a) the artist's originality
   b) the artist's job before he became a painter
   c) the style of the artist's early paintings
   d) the place where the artist first worked

8 In the 1620s, winter scenes painted by Dutch artists were changing in style
   a) by becoming more colourful
   b) by becoming more detailed yet less coloured
   c) by becoming more atmospheric through use of brighter colour
   d) by becoming less preoccupied with small detail and more concerned with overall effect

9 'the prepared ground of the wood panel' (lines 35–6) refers to
   a) the horse-drawn sledge in the picture
   b) the effect of the light on the trees in the picture
   c) the surface on which the picture is painted
   d) the ground beneath the sledge and trees in the picture

10 Which of the following words from the final paragraph does most to sum up the author's view of the style of van Goyen's *Winter Scene*?
   a) spontaneity
   b) prolific
   c) vivid
   d) rapidly executed

Comments on the answers

Now compare how you arrived at your answers with the thoughts and selections below. The correct answer in each case is marked with an asterisk.

1 a) merely an impression based on the picture, whereas the question asks for the subject *according to the passage*.
 b) close reading rejects this one: it is a reference to earlier medieval landscapes (line 10) – not seventeenth-century winter scenes.
 c) contradicted by lines 29–30 which refer to a winter *afternoon*.
 *d) selection depends upon spotting '*in this case* the canals, which froze' (lines 8–9).

2 Given the wording of the question, focus on the first paragraph alone here.
 a) incorrect: the whole paragraph stresses that Dutch art was not grandiose.
 b) yes: the point is made in the opening sentence, where Dutch art is contrasted with Italian art of the period.
 c) wrong: more appropriate to Italian art. (line 3)
 d) obviously wrong as the second half of the paragraph informs us that even 'common farmers' owned paintings.

3 Again, search through paragraph 1 only.
 a) readily confirmed by line 5: Dutch paintings were 'cheap enough'.
 *b) is the exception – yet evidence to contradict in paragraph 1 is confined to lines 8–9: 'the most *popular* subjects reflected the Dutch scene'.
 c) this agrees with the suggestion of 'ordinary things'. (line 4)
 d) amounts to simplification of detail given in the second half of the paragraph.

4 Here you're required to judge the central concern of paragraph 2.
 a) is perhaps true of the first sentence and a half – yet no more than that.
 c) and d) are both given some small attention.
 *b's use of the words 'career' and 'landscape' gives it broader scope and thus makes it the likeliest candidate.

5 d) is unacceptable as it has use of a colon in mind. c) and b) are similar to each other in suggestion and can both be discounted: anything 'less' than a semi-colon would be inadequate separation of the two related elements which the writer wishes to combine in one sentence. Thus *a) is the preferred option.

6 Even if 'insolvent' is unfamiliar to you, the words 'financial trouble' at the end of the preceding sentence are a useful clue, and should dispose of **a)** and possibly **c)**. 'Poor' **d)** is too loose; 'bankrupt' *__b)__ is the synonym required.

7 *__c)__ should be a clear favourite in this case if careful reference back to the previous sentence (lines 21–22) is made. One could sympathise with the mistaken reading that led to the choice of **a)**, yet **b)** and **d)** are crude misinterpretations.

8 This question poses problems in that although **a)** is soon dismissed, both **b)** and **c)** are partially true – but each contains a contradiction. Thorough reading of the third paragraph should give support to alternative *__d)__: 'less diffuse and more unified' (line 27) may prove hard to grasp, but 'overall atmosphere rather than the details' (line 25) is straightforward enough as evidence.

9 The three decoys here (**a)**, **b)** and **d)**) should only tempt those who rely too much on the photograph of the painting. *__c)__ is the correct choice, and should be easily recognised as such if the quotation in the question is read in context. Note the significance of the phrase that follows: 'shine *through* the greyish brushstrokes' (line 36).

10 Process of elimination ought to lead you to discount **b)** 'prolific' as it refers to the artist's output of work and not the painting in question. **c)** and **d)** relate to other drawings that van Goyen made and are not directly relevant. *__a)__, however, refers specifically to *Winter Scene* (NB, '*This* spontaneity' – line 41).

Buried Treasure

Buried treasure has always been a source of eternal speculation and consuming interest. Perhaps it is because everybody enjoys making money and because, in the minds of many, there is a feeling that hidden caches are the easiest way to instant riches. Occasionally this may be so, but usually
5 the trail to a hoard requires intellectual and physical endurance. All too often treasure seekers set off without having done sufficient planning, preparation or research. These form the backbone of treasure seeking, but they must be combined with determination and unwavering belief. Only then can the treasure hunter hope to near his goal.

10 Belief, however, must never become gullibility. The ability to sort out the tiny grains of truth, sifted in painstaking research from the mountains of rumour which surround all tales of buried riches, is an important attribute. As many treasures are found by researching in libraries and museums as by digging in the field with pick and shovel.

15 There are many stories of landlocked treasure. They are classics because of the fabulous wealth involved. Some have been partially discovered by amateurs, and this adds further evidence of their authenticity. There is however a word of caution that is best passed on by recounting a story told by the late and renowned Colonel Fawcett. He recalled hiding £60 of gold
20 that he had previously found when his baggage became overweight on one South American exploration. When he passed by later he was told that an Englishman had come that way and had buried £60,000 of treasure some years before. Of course the glowing accounts made no mention of the fact that he had retrieved the cache later. 'Let would-be treasure hunters ponder
25 the moral of this tale,' he said, and well we ought.

But despite Colonel Fawcett's caution, the treasure seeker should never let his imagination be stifled. Hunting may at times be a soul-destroying business: detractors will often point to the Oak Island Money Pit as proof of the fact that ardent treasure seekers have to spend a fortune and often
30 finish up without any reward. Yet there must be a reason for the overwhelming evidence of treasure on Oak Island and today we have a multitude of technological advantages for finding it. Long and arduous travel is comparatively cheap and easy, equipment is available to buy or hire, and photography, the telephone and the radio allow the determined hunter to
35 check his facts in the field. In short, the treasure seeker of today risks far less than his predecessors and so has a much greater chance of discovering hidden riches. Luck still plays her part, but so she does in any rewarding endeavour, and diligent research is still the key to successful hunting.

To the sceptic I would point out the rewards other than money that are
40 there. Should you find yourself suffering at a desk from any of the commercial sicknesses like nerves, ulcers or simply boredom, you will find that a mild treasure hunt is the greatest therapy in the world – mainly because your objective is never in doubt. The treasure is there and once you have found it your worries will be over.

45 I am not going to claim that treasure seeking is always a quick way to
    riches. Legal wrangles can begin as you try to sell your find. I remember
    meeting the American marine archaeologist and treasure hunter, Robert
    Marx, in 1970 when he was living in Grand Bahama Island. He was just back
    from investigating the sites of the lost Mayan cities in Guatemala. Bob and
50 I went diving over an old Spanish wreck off the Lucayan Beach where a large
    collection of Spanish silver coins had been discovered some eighteen months
    previously. I was told that the lucky finders had become involved in a legal
    case and would be fortunate if ownership of the haul was eventually settled
    on them. At that time the coins were in a bank vault in Freeport, and when
55 I left in September 1971, they had only just been released for sale.
        So if you know a little about the law, have a working knowledge of
    geology, history and archaeology combined with the rudiments of map-
    reading, secret languages and perhaps a smattering of mining engineering,
    you are ready for the treasure hunt. There is no doubt in my mind that there
60 is still plenty there for the taking.

Buried Treasure Roy Norvill

Multiple choice comprehension

1 A 'consuming interest' (line 2) is best
described as an interest which
  a) takes up much time and attention
  b) is expensive to follow
  c) requires complete dedication
  d) is likely to yield a profit

2 The writer's explanation in lines 2–4 of the
popularity of buried treasure is
  a) questioned
  b) implied
  c) proved
  d) suggested

3 In having an 'unwavering belief' (line 8),
treasure seekers must
  a) never doubt for one moment that they will
     find treasure
  b) trust in their judgement that their calcu-
     lations are correct
  c) hope for the best that treasure will turn up
  d) not confide in others but keep their inner-
     most thoughts to themselves

4 The writer mentions all the following characteristics of a successful treasure seeker *except*
the need to be
  a) resolute
  b) confident
  c) persistent
  d) secretive

5 In the first paragraph the writer's criticism of
treasure seekers is that they are
  a) lazy
  b) indecisive
  c) easily fooled
  d) ill-equipped

6 'attribute' (line 12) is nearest in meaning to
  a) quality
  b) talent
  c) acquisition
  d) technique

7 In the second paragraph it is indicated that a would-be treasure seeker needs qualities and skills similar to those of a
  a) detective
  b) student
  c) lawyer
  d) librarian

8 The story told by Colonel Fawcett (lines 19–25) shows the part played by
  a) deceit
  b) greed
  c) rumour
  d) fraud

9 'glowing accounts' (line 23) are accounts which
  a) are designed to mislead the unwary
  b) throw light on an important truth
  c) tend to exaggerate the facts
  d) would be taken seriously by experts

10 As used in line 24 'ponder' is nearest in meaning to
  a) take to heart
  b) bear in mind
  c) commit to memory
  d) give thought to

11 In regard to Colonel Fawcett's advice, the writer
  a) expresses approval
  b) makes no comment
  c) appears lukewarm
  d) doubts its value

12 In lines 26–27 the writer states that a treasure seeker should have
  a) confidence to indulge his fancies
  b) determination to plan his future
  c) courage to throw off restraint
  d) perseverance to exploit his potential

13 According to the 'detractors' (line 28)
  a) money in the bank is better than treasure in the ground
  b) the road to bankruptcy is paved with unfound treasure
  c) spending money is no guarantee of finding treasure
  d) hope may spring eternal, but treasure seekers will find despair

14 The writer states that on Oak Island there
  a) is still some more treasure to be found
  b) has been treasure which has previously been recovered
  c) should be treasure which new techniques may find
  d) has been neither treasure nor hope of finding any

15 According to the writer, 'a multitude of technological advantages' (lines 31–32)
  a) guarantees success in the operation
  b) lessens the risk of complete failure
  c) makes treasure easier to locate
  d) gives greater confidence to the seeker

16 The writer suggests that modern technology not only gives the treasure seeker more hope of success, but also
  a) provides him with easier rewards
  b) reduces his dependence on luck
  c) economises on manpower
  d) makes the expedition less dangerous

17 As used in line 39 a 'sceptic' is a person who
  a) casts doubt
  b) rejects out of hand
  c) has utter contempt for
  d) has no interest in

18 The writer argues that 'a mild treasure hunt' (line 42) will
  a) make you feel better by providing a fixed goal
  b) arouse your excitement by offering a new challenge
  c) give you an incentive by showing an interesting prospect
  d) improve your physical health by engaging your mental powers

19 Which one of the following words is nearest in meaning to 'wrangles' as used in line 46?
  a) swindles
  b) disputes
  c) proceedings
  d) manoeuvres

20 The writer appears to mention his meeting with Robert Marx (line 47) specifically to
  a) show that he knows a genuine treasure hunter
  b) give a hint that the lost Mayan cities contained treasure
  c) illustrate the fact that treasure can be found at sea
  d) introduce an example of delay in proving ownership of treasure

21 Which one of the following words is nearest in meaning to 'sites' as used in line 49?
  a) views
  b) locations
  c) surroundings
  d) features

22 Lucayan Beach (line 50) is
  a) in Guatemala
  b) on Grand Bahama Island
  c) one of the lost Mayan cities
  d) in Spain

23 In referring to the legal case (line 52), the writer wants to show that
  a) ownership has to be established beyond any doubt
  b) the original owners of treasure can stake a claim
  c) banks are reluctant to give up their hold
  d) proving ownership of treasure can take a long time

24 A 'knowledge of geology' (line 56) would help a treasure hunter decide
  a) where treasure could have been buried
  b) which countries could have hidden treasure
  c) where wrecks could have sunk
  d) how treasure could have been found

25 In the course of the passage the writer expresses all of the following ideas *except* that
  a) easy riches can be obtained from treasure hunting
  b) treasure hunting offers more than the chance of wealth
  c) technology has eased the task of the treasure hunter
  d) shipwrecks are the most likely source of wealth

AEB *Section II*

Their House

To the boy the entire house was an adventure where nothing could possibly
go wrong. His mother and grandmother enfolded him often, the house all
the time, from early rising until he returned to smooth sheets and the faint
fragrance of lavender. It was only afterwards, a long time afterwards, that
5   he realised how much the house depended upon the two women, and the
other one – his grandfather – who rose six hours before the rest and went
soundlessly out to ride at the end of the dancing rope and return in mid-
morning with the coal dust thick upon his skin and heavy as bee's pollen on
his eyelashes.

10   But at the moment what mattered was the marvellous adventure of the
house – much bigger than the one they had left – with its succession of
rooms. He compared the house in his mind to a shell, not the dumpy little
shells of the hedgerow snails, but one of the big conch shells that guarded
the top of the rockery; an unfolding spiral of cosy pink rooms all centred
15   on the kitchen with its prodded mat, steel fender and snapping fire. And he
had the free run of it all. After the two-roomed cottage by the riverside it
was a palace. At first he'd missed the busy little tankies which ran right up
the front street, hissing, snorting and thrusting the loaded coal wagons with
all their might and main. He'd missed the tankies more than he'd missed the
20   big red-haired man, the one who'd come in day after day as black as
Grandad. This one had bathed in front of the fire and his splutterings had
been an intrusion. He hadn't liked the way he said 'My back!' or the way
his mother responded by rubbing the flannel over with the flat of her hand,
kneeling beside the man, until the lather was white and clean then pouring
25   over the clean warm water until she could use the towel. They'd laughed
together and he'd watch. At those times his mother seemed to forget him.
It was like watching through a window but worse because there was no glass.

That hadn't happened for a long time. Not since the day a big red-faced
man had knocked at the door. The man had a very quiet voice, and when
30   he carried his mother to the sofa the boy had noticed the brass-buckle of
his belt at the middle of his back. Even although he was afraid for his mother
he'd wondered why the belt was fastened at the back. And then the women
had come flocking in and the big man had taken him by the hand and said,
'Come, lad, let's go for a walk.'
35   'Ah want to stay wi' me mother,' he whimpered, and fat old Grandma
Martin – she was Grandma to everybody in the village – had said, 'Now,
honey, the nice man'll show ye the river-dogs if ye go quick.' So he'd gone,
but not before he'd seen the four men with their burden walking unsteadily
down the sleepers between the railway lines. Beyond he'd seen the men and
40   lads filing down the gangway with the dead midgie lamps flapping in their
jacket lapels.

He knew it wasn't the right time for the men to ride – the buzzer always
blew first. 'Mister, look!' he said. 'Look at all the men.'

'Come on, son,' said the man. 'Else we'll miss the river-dogs.'

45   'But the men – is there no more coal?'

'The pit's idle, Ah reckon,' said the man with an uneasy laugh.

'Those men carrying – are they takin' something to *our* house?'

'God help us wi' all these questions,' said the big man and wiped his face with a red hankie. 'It's only some chaps carrying a part – a part for the

50   tankies,' he concluded triumphantly.

'Poor men,' said the boy. 'No caps.'

'It's a hot day, why should they wear caps!' said the big man, and took his hand and hurt him until they reached the tall stems of the blind men's baccy. 'Now, quiet,' he said. 'Them dogs is shy.'

55   They watched and watched but the dogs didn't come out.

'Do you believe in river-dogs, Mam?' he said that night. 'The big man took me to the river but they didn't come out – he said they smelt us.'

But his Mam hadn't said anything. She'd sat in front of the fire and played with the poker. And Grandma Martin had said: 'Poor lamb,' and his mother

60   had started crying; he'd felt the tears drop on his hands where she held them in her lap. The tears were hot.

A time after Grandma Martin had said: 'Come and see your father.'

She took him into the bedroom and he looked at the iron bedstead, expecting to see his father. But his father wasn't there. Grandma Martin

65   lifted him up in her arms. 'There he is,' she said softly. 'He's sleeping, so just say goodbye to him.'

'Goodbye, father,' he said.

'He'll never wake,' said Grandma Martin.

'Did Mam wash his back?' he asked.

70   'God have mercy,' said Grandma Martin and carried him back to the kitchen.

Next to the nice smell of the many rooms the immensely comforting thing about his grandfather's house was that his mother was his alone; the two old people belonged to him also, entirely. You never looked through glass. The

75   four of us are happy together, he often used to think.

The Bachelor Uncle Sid Chaplin

Multiple choice comprehension

1 'To the boy the house was an adventure where nothing could go wrong' (lines 1–2) because
   a) he felt safe, knowing his way around the house so well
   b) he was extremely careful in moving around the house
   c) he was constantly supervised by his mother and grandmother

   d) the familiar house and the attentions of his mother and grandmother made him feel secure

2 'enfolded' as used in the passage (line 2) means
   a) comforted
   b) kissed
   c) wrapped
   d) surrounded

3 'It was only . . . a long time afterwards, that he realised how much the house depended upon the two women, and . . . his grandfather' (lines 4–6) suggests
- **a)** the boy was thoughtless
- **b)** the boy cared little for his guardians
- **c)** the boy was too young to fully appreciate their efforts
- **d)** at the time two of the adults did little towards the upkeep of the house

4 Paragraph one informs us that the boy's grandfather works
- **a)** delivering coal with a horse-drawn cart
- **b)** as a ropemaker
- **c)** as a bee keeper
- **d)** as a coal miner

5 Which one of the following does *not* apply to the new house?
- **a)** pleasant-smelling
- **b)** situated by the river
- **c)** the kitchen was at the heart of the house
- **d)** it had a rockery

6 'heavy as bee's pollen' (line 8) is
- **a)** a metaphor
- **b)** a simile
- **c)** an example of personification
- **d)** an example of alliteration

7 The main reason for comparing the new house to a conch shell (paragraph 2) is
- **a)** the pink colouring of the rooms
- **b)** the conical shape of the building
- **c)** the layout of the house's rooms in relation to the kitchen
- **d)** the spiral staircase in the house

8 Which of the following most accurately describes the boy's feelings when he recalls times when his mother used to bathe his father?
- **a)** fond remembrance
- **b)** jealousy
- **c)** indifference
- **d)** sadness

9 The boy goes on a walk with the big red-faced man because
- **a)** the outing has been arranged for some time
- **b)** the adults wish him out of the house at such a difficult time
- **c)** he wished to escape from the uncomfortable atmosphere of the house
- **d)** searching for river-dogs was a favourite pastime

10 The expression 'It was like watching through a window' (line 27) suggests
- **a)** the boy's vision was blurred by tears
- **b)** he felt like a mere onlooker at such times
- **c)** it was a strange feeling thinking back to times spent with his father
- **d)** he was spying on his parents

11 The boy *first* realises that something is amiss at the pit
- **a)** when he sees men on the railway line with their lamps out
- **b)** when he sees men on the line although the buzzer hasn't sounded for them to emerge
- **c)** when he notices the men are not wearing their hats
- **d)** because the tankies are not running

12 'concluded triumphantly' (line 50) means that the red-faced man
- **a)** had at last worked out what the four men were carrying
- **b)** enjoyed proving that the boy's observation was incorrect
- **c)** was pleased at finding a means to explain away the boy's question
- **d)** was delighted that the replacement part for the tankie had at last been obtained

13 All the following describe the red-faced man's reactions to the boy, whilst they were walking, *except*
  a) anxious embarrassment
  b) tactlessness
  c) urgency
  d) impatience

14 The men on the line are not wearing caps because
  a) as the boy suggests, they are poor and cannot afford them
  b) as the man suggests, the weather is too hot
  c) being miners, they would wear helmets and not hats
  d) it is a convention to remove headwear when someone has died

15 When the boy talks to his mother on returning, she doesn't answer because
  a) she is busy tending to the fire
  b) she is not interested in river-dogs
  c) she is preoccupied and therefore silent
  d) Grandma Martin interrupts before his mother can reply

16 The sentence 'But his father wasn't there.' (line 64)
  a) tells us that the boy's father had got out of bed
  b) confirms our suspicion that the boy's father is dead
  c) indicates that the boy is too small to get a clear view of what is on the bed
  d) tells us that his father's appearance is greatly changed and that the boy doesn't recognise him at first

17 All the following remarks by the boy are included to stress his lack of understanding of events *except*
  a) 'Did Mam wash his back?' (line 69)
  b) '. . . are they takin' something to *our* house?' (line 47)
  c) 'But the men – is there no more coal?' (line 45)
  d) 'Mister, look! Look at all the men.' (line 43)

18 Grandma Martin says 'God have mercy' (line 70)
  a) because she is taken aback by the boy's question
  b) as a mark of respect for the dead man
  c) because she fears for the future of the boy's family
  d) because events in the kitchen have caught her attention

19 Grandma Martin's attitude towards the boy is
  a) painstaking
  b) sympathetic
  c) explanatory
  d) submissive

20 Which of the following extracts comes closest to summarising the passage as a whole?
  a) 'Next to the nice smell of the many rooms the immensely comforting thing about his grandfather's house was that his mother was his alone; the two old people belonged to him also, entirely.' (lines 72–74)
  b) 'You never looked through glass. The four of us are happy, together . . .'(lines 74–75)
  c) '"He'll never wake," said Grandma Martin.' (line 68)
  d) 'what mattered was the marvellous adventure of the house' (line 10)

The Investment Dynamos

We used to play twice a month, at Upland Park or at our opponents' pitch, but Upland Park was what we laughingly called our 'home ground'. Twice or three times a month too we'd meet after work or on Saturday mornings for 'training'. But the whole business was meant to be a joke. We said we'd
5   quit if we found things becoming serious.

We worked in an office in the Investments Branch – a long, murmuring office with dull-bright polished surfaces – recording the financial jugglery an insurance company employs to maintain its funds. Penpushers in a word. Men who leant at desks, muttered into telephones, emptied and filled wire
10   trays; were regarded as fixtures by a company which paid them no particular honours for it; more than half way through life and a little under half way up the ladder of promotion, which meant that at our age – undisguisable middle age – some of the upper rungs might as well have been sawn off. That truncated ladder was the vital thing. If it hadn't been for our sense of those
15   sawn off rungs, of rungs of ladders – of which the company one perhaps was the least important – ladders involving wives and families, ladders gauging the wisdom we had to offer our children, the trust we had to place in ourselves, we might never have started that football team. There comes a time when a gesture of congratulatory self-mockery, if it is to be made at
20   all, had better be made at once before the joke actually loses its humour.

Word had filtered through that other branches and other firms in other corners of the city were turning out football teams of middle-aged drudges, and perhaps it was clear from our very scoffing that we should do the same. We had slack shoulders, flabby arms, pot bellies, double chins, weak knees.
25   There was the usual argument of keeping fit which nags those who believe they have not climbed all the rungs. But something deeper induces a body of unathletic over-forties to don shorts and football boots. Was it the thought of matching the sober absurdities of our desk-life with something more brazenly absurd? Or was it something less wry, altogether more wistful, that
30   resolved us that wet Friday lunch-time when Mitchell said, his podgy face colouring slightly over his thermos flask, 'Well why not?' and it no longer seemed a question one could answer?

It was meant as a joke. We were open to ridicule which we could only forestall by laughing at ourselves and we were not going to fall into the trap
35   of our age of waxing earnest over our follies. We called ourselves the Investment Dynamos, and were deliberately undynamic. Our first match had to be postponed two hours because we failed to book a pitch from the park-keeper. We liked to be known as 'gentlemen' not 'amateur' players. We bought or acquired a motley collection of kit – lurid tee-shirts, stretched cast-
40   offs of sons at school – and deliberately shunned the uniform colours of teams we played so as to keep our enthusiasm in proportion. But we were not immune, after the first aches and gasps, to a sense of physical elation. Those frosty Saturdays when we shivered in our shorts and the rime on the outspread pitches smoked and turned to dew under the sun were wonderful

45 times to us sedentaries, who normally at such times would be beginning desultory, lacklustre weekends, fetching shopping, buying lunchtime beers, cocooned from the elements by cars and cardigans. The sensations of actually doing, shamblingly albeit, what men of our age normally did not were gratifying; and the smiles which crossed our panting faces in the
50 changing rooms were less those of a joke carried through than of capacities rediscovered.

Drew Graham Swift

Multiple choice comprehension

1 Upland Park is 'laughingly' referred to as a 'home ground' because
  a) the pitch is in appalling condition
  b) where they play is no more than a pitch in a local park
  c) the pitch has no stadium for spectators
  d) later in the passage we are told they once failed to book the pitch

2 The word or phrase which could best take the place of 'fixtures' (line 10) is
  a) permanent objects
  b) incompetent
  c) games arranged
  d) bores

3 The main idea of the second paragraph is
  a) that the men were dissatisfied with their lack of promotion at work
  b) that being middle-aged it was ridiculous to take up football
  c) that the men were bored by the work that they had to do
  d) that because of their middle-aged self-doubts it was timely to form a football team as a joke at their own expense

4 The passage suggests that the men in the Investments Branch decided to start a football team for all of the following reasons *except*
  a) because other firms were forming football teams of middle-aged employees
  b) because they were sure that they could beat the other middle-aged teams
  c) because some of the men felt that it would be a means of maintaining fitness
  d) because it would be an activity even more ridiculous than their office jobs

5 'forestall' (line 34) is most accurately replaced by
  a) complement
  b) prevent
  c) echo
  d) pre-empt

6 The Investment Dynamos were 'deliberately undynamic' because
  a) their skill as footballers made undue exertion unnecessary
  b) they realised that over-exertion could be dangerous at their age
  c) they were determined not to take their football too seriously
  d) as gentlemen players they disapproved of a crude, energetic style of football

79

7 The Investment Dynamos 'shunned uniform colours' because

   a) it was pointless to lavish money on an expensive team strip

   b) the players' families insisted on providing them with old or cast-off kit

   c) this meant that they never risked the confusion of appearing in the same colours at their opponents

   d) their motley kit was in keeping with the desire to laugh at themselves

8 The sense of *winter* Saturdays, introduced by 'frosty' (line 43) is reinforced by all the following *except*

   a) 'we shivered in our shorts' (line 43)

   b) 'rime . . . on the pitches . . . smoked . . . under the sun' (lines 43–44)

   c) 'desultory . . . weekends' (line 46)

   d) 'cocooned from the elements' (line 47)

9 The sort of weekends that the men spent before taking up football might best be described as

   a) disjointed and unexciting

   b) comfortable and thus enjoyable

   c) entertaining yet demanding

   d) housebound and inconsequential

10 The final sentence of the passage is mainly concerned to

   a) picture the team's elation, smiling in victory over their opponents

   b) stress a sense of rejuvenation that playing football gave the team

   c) show the team mocking their own shambling efforts after the match

   d) show the relief on the players' faces at having completed another exhausting game

Oral work

1 In groups of four or five, improvise a family tea-time scene in the home of Mitchell, a founder member of the Investment Dynamos, on the evening that he announces his decision to play football again at the age of forty-five.

2 Discuss the view that the middle-aged ought to keep their 'flab' under cover rather than take up energetic pursuits such as jogging, squash and other sports.

Further written work

3 Write a humorous newspaper report about one of the Investment Dynamos' matches, including an eye-catching headline and sub-headings.

4 Describe in detail a member of the Investment Dynamos, captured in action by a series of close-up camera shots at different times before, during, and after a game.

Long comprehensions

Mother and Daughters

In the following extract Binny is the mother and Lucy (18 years) and Alison (11 years) are her children. Binny is preparing for a small dinner party and has arranged for the girls to sleep at a neighbour's home. She has just told Alison to come down from upstairs.

'Alison won't,' said Lucy, coming back into the room.

'Well, make her,' shouted Binny, stamping her foot. She was beginning to breathe quite heavily. 'I would be grateful if you would get your own things together as well. Have you got your nightdress?'

5   'Don't be bloody wet,' said Lucy. She went to the table and tore at a french loaf with her teeth.

'I don't want to remind you of the shirt I bought you,' Binny said. 'Or the pair of shoes costing twenty-four pounds that you said you couldn't live without and promptly gave to your friend Soggy. When I was your age I was

10   grateful if my mother gave me a smile.'

'I lent them, you fool,' corrected Lucy.

Binny's voice became shrill. 'I've long since given up expecting gratitude or common courtesy, but I do expect you to get Alison and yourself out of the house. It's little enough to ask, God knows.'

15   'Keep your lid on,' said Lucy. She began to comb her hair at the mirror. Strands of hair and crumbs of bread fell to the hearth. Binny could feel a pulse beating in her throat. She burned with fury. No wonder she never put on an ounce of weight. The daily aggravation the children caused her was probably comparable to a five-mile run or an hour with the skipping rope.

20   Clutching the region of her heart and fighting for self-control, she said insincerely, 'Darling, you can be very sensitive and persuasive. Just tell her Sybil's waiting and that there's ice cream and things.'

Lucy strolled into the hall and called loudly, 'Come down, Alison, or I'll bash your teeth in.'

25   After several minutes a sound of barking was heard on the first-floor landing.

'Baby,' crooned Binny, going upstairs with outstretched arms. Alison was on all fours, crouched against the wall. Binny often told friends it was nothing to worry about. Until two years ago Alison had insisted on baring

30   her tummy button in the street and rubbing it against lamp posts. She had grown out of that, as doubtless she would soon grow tired of pretending she was a dog.

'Come along, darling,' said Binny brightly. She bent down and patted her daughter's head.

35   Alison growled and seized Binny's ankle in her teeth.

Putting both hands behind her to resist hitting the child, Binny descended the stairs.

Lucy was at the sink pouring cooking sherry into a milk bottle.

'Out, out, out,' cried Binny. 'I am not here to provide booze for your
40 layabout friends. This is not an off-licence.'

She frogmarched Lucy to the door and pushed her down the steps. Alison began to cry. Running down the path, Binny caught up with Lucy at the hedge and put desperate arms about her. She said urgently, 'Now please, pull yourself together. Get your things, take your coat, and I'll give you a
45 pound note to spend.'

Smirking, Lucy re-entered the house and began to put on her flying jacket. Smothering her youngest daughter in kisses, Binny took her to the door. She nodded blindly as Alison climbed the fence.

'You're crying, Mummy,' called Alison. Her mouth quivered.
50 'I'm very happy, darling,' said Binny. 'Don't you worry about me.' She wiped her cheeks with her hands. 'I'm going to have a lovely party.' She stood there waving until Alison was let into the Evans's.

Injury Time Beryl Bainbridge

Comprehension

1 What do the following words tell us about the individuals to whom they are applied?
a) shrill (line 12)
b) insincerely (line 21)
c) frogmarched (line 41)
d) smirking (line 46) (8)

2 What is odd about Alison's behaviour? (3) Quote the words that show that Binny realises that it was odd.

3 Give a character study of Lucy based (8) on her actions and language in this passage.

4 Describe fully the relationship between (11) Binny and her children and try to account for the inconsistency of it.

Total (30)

Further written work

5 Concentrating on revealing the characters through their conversation, trace the development of a family argument basing your writing on personal experience.

6 Write out an extensive description of a young person wanting to seem older and an older person trying to look young. They may be separate descriptions or connected.

Discussion

7 On what topics do you find the greatest difference of opinion between
a) mothers and daughters
b) mothers and sons
c) fathers and daughters
d) fathers and sons
e) brothers and sisters?

8 Because all parents and children are of different generations, do you think it inevitable that there will always be rows and arguments between them?

9 How can each side of the generation gap appreciate the other side's point of view?

A Teacher Gets His Gun

I told the boys to stay quiet while I went to fetch my gun.

It usually worked. For the five minutes that it took me to get to the locker in the common-room and to return to the classroom thirty fourteen-year-old semi-repressed hooligans could be counted on to be held in a state of fragile
5 good behaviour, restrained only by the promise of a lesson they'd actually looked forward to. Physics in general they took to be unacceptably hard mental labour, but what happened when a gun spat out a bullet . . . that was interesting.

Jenkins delayed me for a moment in the common-room: Jenkins with his
10 sour expression and bad-tempered moustache, telling me I could teach momentum more clearly with chalk on a blackboard, and that an actual firearm was on my part simply self-indulgent dramatics.

'No doubt you're right,' I said blandly, edging round him.

He gave me his usual look of frustrated spite. He hated my policy of
15 always agreeing with him, which was, of course, why I did it.

'Excuse me,' I said, retreating, 'Four A are waiting.'

Four A, however, weren't waiting in the hoped-for state of gently simmering excitement. They were, instead, in collective giggles fast approaching mild hysteria.
20 'Look,' I said flatly, sensing the atmosphere with one foot through the door, 'steady down, or you'll copy notes . . .'

This direst of threats had no result. The giggles couldn't be stifled. The eyes of the class darted between me and my gun and the blackboard, which was still out of my sight behind the open door, and upon every young face
25 there was the most gleeful anticipation.

'OK,' I said, closing the door, 'so what have you writ . . .'

I stopped.

They hadn't written anything.

One of the boys stood there, in front of the blackboard, straight and still:
30 Paul Arcady, the wit of the class. He stood straight and still because, balanced on his head, there was an apple.

The giggles all around me exploded into laughter, and I couldn't myself keep a straight face.

'Can you shoot it off, sir?'
35 The voices rose above a general hubbub.

'William Tell could, sir.'

'Shall we call an ambulance, sir, just in case?'

'How long will it take a bullet to get through Paul's skull, sir?'

'Very funny,' I said repressively, but indeed it was very funny and they
40 knew it. But if I laughed too much I'd lose control of them, and control of such a volatile mass was always precarious.

'Very clever, Paul,' I said. 'Go and sit down.'

He was satisfied. He'd produced his effect perfectly. He took the apple off his head with a natural elegance and returned in good order to his place,

45   accepting as his due the admiring jokes and the envious catcalls.

'Right then,' I said, planting myself firmly where he had stood, 'by the end of this lesson you'll all know how long it would take for a bullet travelling at a certain speed to cross a certain distance . . .'

50   The gun I had taken to the lesson had been a simple air gun, but I told them also how a rifle worked, and why in each case a bullet or a pellet came out fast. I let them handle the smooth metal: the first time many of them had seen an actual gun, even an air gun, at close quarters. I explained how bullets were made, and how they differed from the pellets I had with me. How loading mechanisms worked. How the grooves inside a rifle barrel

55   rotated the bullet, to send it out spinning. I told them about air friction, and heat.

They listened with concentration and asked the questions they always did.

'Can you tell us how a bomb works, sir?'

'One day,' I said.

60   'A nuclear bomb?'

'One day.'

'A hydrogen . . . cobalt . . . neutron bomb?'

'One day.'

They never asked how radio waves crossed the ether, which was to me

65   a greater mystery. They asked about destruction, not creation; about power, not symmetry. The seed of violence born in every male child looked out of every face, and I knew how they were thinking, because I'd been there myself. Why else had I spent countless hours at their age practising with a .22 cadet rifle on a range, improving my skill until I could hit a target the

70   size of a thumbnail at fifty yards, nine times out of ten. A strange, pointless, sublimated skill, which I never intended to use on any living creature, but had never since lost.

'Is it true, sir,' one of them said, 'that you won an Olympic medal for rifle shooting?'

75   'No, it isn't.'

'What, then, sir?'

'I want you all to consider the speed of a bullet compared to the speed of other objects you are all familiar with. Now, do you think that you could be flying along in an aeroplane, and look out of the window, and see a bullet

80   keeping pace with you, appearing to be standing still just outside the window?'

The lesson wound on. They would remember it all their lives, because of the gun. Without the gun, whatever Jenkins might think, it would have faded into the general dust they shook from their shoes every afternoon at four

85   o'clock. Teaching, it often seemed to me, was as much a matter of image-jerking as of imparting actual information. The facts dressed up in jokes were the ones they got right in exams.

Twice Shy Dick Francis

Comprehension

1 Explain clearly and in your own words what the author means by the following:
   a) in a state of fragile good behaviour (line 4)
   b) self-indulgent dramatics (line 12)
   c) blandly (line 13)
   d) facts dressed up in jokes (line 86)   (6)

2 'control of such a volatile mass was always precarious'. (lines 40–41)
   a) Explain this in your own words.   (2)
   b) In what way is the wording appropriate to the speaker?   (2)

3 What evidence is there of the class's attitude towards physics?   (2)

4 In not more than three or four lines comment on the joke played by the boys.   (3)

5 Describe the attitude of the boys towards their teacher, paying particular attention to their questions and answers.   (4)

6 Would you say that it was a successful lesson? Give reasons for your answer. What qualities as a teacher does the writer show?   (6)

Total (25)

Further work

7 The opening sentence is quite startling (and is a good example for your own essay or story writing). However it is often difficult to maintain the interest created by such an opening. How does the author try to do this and how successful is he?

8 Study carefully the use of conversation.
   a) Give examples which show how it carries along the story line or reveals incidents.
   b) Give examples which show how it helps to reveal the character of the speaker.

9 The other teacher, Jenkins, is referred to twice in the extract.
   a) Describe briefly the type of lesson you think Jenkins would give.
   b) What is his attitude towards the author? Quote from the passage in support.
   c) What does the reference to Jenkins at the end of the passage tell us about the author's confidence in the lesson he has just given?
   d) What contrast is there between Jenkins and the author?

10 The technique of establishing one character by contrast with another is common in fiction and plays. Often it is done by placing one character in a situation and another character in a similar situation and examining them, so showing the difference in the way they behave. If you are studying one of the following Shakespeare plays say how Shakespeare uses this in order to create the characters.

   a) *Henry IV Part I*
      Hotspur and Falstaff
      Hotspur and Hal
      Hal and Falstaff
      King Henry and Hal

   b) *Romeo and Juliet*
      Juliet and the Nurse
      Romeo and Tybalt
      The Nurse and Friar Lawrence
      Mercutio and Romeo

   c) *MacBeth*
      MacBeth and Banquo
      MacBeth and Lady MacBeth
      MacBeth and Macduff
      Lady MacBeth and Malcolm
      The visions arising from MacBeth's state of mind and those arising outside of him.

   d) *Julius Caesar*
      Calpurnia and Portia
      Cassius and Brutus
      Brutus and Mark Antony
      Caesar's Body and the Spirit of Caesar

A Maths Lesson?

'This morning,' I remarked, taking up my *Hall and Knight*, 'we will do problems,' and I told them at once that if there was any more of that groaning they would do nothing but problems for the next month. It is my experience, as an assistant master of some years' standing, that if groaning is not checked
5   immediately it may swell to enormous proportions. I make it my business to stamp on it.

Mason, a fair-haired boy with glasses, remarked when the groaning had died down that it would not be possible to do problems for the next month, and on being asked why not, replied that there were only three weeks more
10   of term. This is true, and I decided to make no reply. He then asked if he could have a mark for that. I said, 'No, Mason, you may not,' and, taking up my book and a piece of chalk, read out, 'I am just half as old as my father and in twenty years I shall be five years older than he was twenty years ago. How old am I?' Atkins promptly replied, 'Forty-two.' I inquired of him how,
15   unless he was gifted with supernatural powers, he imagined he could produce the answer without troubling to do any working out. He said, 'I saw it in the School's year-book.' This stupid reply caused a great deal of laughter, which I suppressed.

I should have spoken sharply to Atkins, but at this moment I noticed that
20   his neighbour, Sapoulos, the Greek boy, appeared to be eating toffee, a practice which is forbidden at Burgrove during school hours. I ordered him to stand up. 'Sapoulos,' I said, 'you are not perhaps quite used yet to our English ways, and I shall not punish you this time for your disobedience; but please understand that I will not have eating in my class. You did not come
25   here to eat but to learn. If you try hard and pay attention, I do not altogether despair of teaching you something, but if you do not wish to learn I cannot help you. You might as well go back to your own country.' Mason, without being given permission to speak, cried excitedly, 'He can't, sir. Didn't you know? His father was chased out of Greece in a revolution or something.
30   A big man with a black beard chased him for three miles and he had to escape in a small boat. It's true, sir. You ask him. Sapoulos got hit on the knee with a brick, didn't you Sappy? And his grandmother – at least I think it was his grandmother –'

'That will do, Mason,' I said. 'Who threw that?'
35   I am not, I hope, a martinet, but I will not tolerate the throwing of paper darts, or other missiles in my algebra set. Some of the boys make small pellets out of their blotting paper and flick them with their garters. This sort of thing has to be put down with a firm hand or work becomes impossible. I accordingly warned the boy responsible that another offence would mean
40   an imposition. He had the impertinence to ask what sort of an imposition. I said that it would be a pretty stiff imposition, and if he wished to know more exact details he had only to throw another dart to find out. He thereupon threw another dart.

45 I confess that at this I lost patience and threatened to keep the whole set in during the afternoon if I had any more trouble. The lesson then proceeded.

It was not until I had completed my working out of the problem on the board that I realised I had worked on the assumption – of course ridiculous – that I was twice my father's age instead of half. This gave the false figure

50 of minus ninety for my own age. Some boy said, 'Crikey!' I at once whipped round and demanded to know who had spoken. Otterway suggested that it might have been Hopgood talking in his sleep. I was about to reprimand Otterway for impertinence when I realised that Hopgood actually was asleep and had in fact, according to Williamson, been asleep since the beginning

55 of the period. Mason said, 'He hasn't missed much, anyway.'

I then threw my *Hall and Knight*.

A J Wentworth B.A. H Ellis

Comprehension

1 Quote 3 statements the teacher makes when he tries to assert his authority. What happens immediately afterwards? (6)

2 Describe the attitude of the boys towards him and support your points with reference to the text. (5)

3 How good was the teacher at keeping
a) discipline in class
b) the interest of the class?
Support your answer with references. (4)

4 Write out a character sketch of the teacher both as a person and as a teacher. (5)

5 Continue the extract for 15 to 20 lines. (10)

Total (30)

The Importance of Being Earnest

LADY BRACKNELL   Good afternoon, dear Algernon, I hope you are behaving very well.

ALGERNON   I'm feeling very well, Aunt Augusta.

LADY BRACKNELL   That's not quite the same thing. In fact the two things
5   rarely go together. (*Sees JACK and bows to him with icy coldness.*)

ALGERNON (*to GWENDOLEN*) Dear me, you are smart!

GWENDOLEN   I am always smart! Aren't I, Mr Worthing?

JACK   You're quite perfect, Miss Fairfax.

GWENDOLEN   Oh! I hope I am not that. It would leave no room for
10   developments, and I intend to develop in many directions. (*GWENDOLEN and JACK sit down together in the corner.*)

LADY BRACKNELL   I'm sorry if we are a little late, Algernon, but I was obliged to call on dear Lady Harbury. I hadn't been there since her poor husband's death. I never saw a woman so altered; she looks quite twenty
15   years younger. And now I'll have a cup of tea, and one of those nice cucumber sandwiches you promised me.

ALGERNON   Certainly, Aunt Augusta. (*Goes over to tea-table.*)

LADY BRACKNELL   Won't you come and sit here, Gwendolen?

GWENDOLEN   Thanks, mamma, I'm quite comfortable where I am.

20   ALGERNON (*picking up empty plate in horror*)   Good heavens! Lane! Why are there no cucumber sandwiches? I ordered them specially.

LANE (*gravely*) There were no cucumbers in the market this morning, sir.
I went down twice.

ALGERNON   No cucumbers!

25   LANE   No, sir. Not even for ready money.

ALGERNON   That will do, Lane, thank you.

LANE   Thank you, sir.

ALGERNON   I am greatly distressed, Aunt Augusta, about there being no cucumbers, not even for ready money.

30   LADY BRACKNELL   It really makes no matter, Algernon. I had some crumpets with Lady Harbury, who seems to me to be living entirely for pleasure now.

ALGERNON   I hear her hair has turned quite gold from grief.

LADY BRACKNELL   It certainly has changed its colour. From what cause
35   I, of course, cannot say. (*ALGERNON crosses and hands tea.*) Thank you. I've quite a treat for you to-night, Algernon. I am going to send you down* with Mary Farquhar. She is such a nice woman, and so attentive to her husband. It's delightful to watch them.

ALGERNON   I am afraid, Aunt Augusta, I shall have to give up the pleasure
40   of dining with you tonight after all.

LADY BRACKNELL   (*frowning*) I hope not, Algernon. It would put my

---

* i.e. sit next to at dinner.

table completely out. Your uncle would have to dine upstairs. Fortunately he is accustomed to that.

ALGERNON   It is a great bore, and, I need hardly say, a terrible disap-
pointment to me, but the fact is I have just had a telegram to say that my poor friend Bunbury is very ill again. (*Exchanges glances with JACK.*) They seem to think I should be with him.

LADY BRACKNELL   It is very strange. This Mr Bunbury seems to suffer from curiously bad health.

ALGERNON   Yes; poor Bunbury is a dreadful invalid.

LADY BRACKNELL   Well, I must say, Algernon, that I think it is high time that Mr Bunbury made up his mind whether he was going to live or die. This shilly-shallying with the question is absurd. Nor do I in any way approve of the modern sympathy with invalids. I consider it morbid. Illness of any kind is hardly a thing to be encouraged in others. Health is the primary duty of life. I am always telling that to your poor uncle, but he never seems to take much notice . . . as far as any improvement in his ailments goes. I should be obliged if you would ask Mr Bunbury, from me, to be kind enough not to have a relapse on Saturday, for I rely on you to arrange my music for me. It is my last reception, and one wants something that will encourage conversation, particularly at the end of the season when everyone has practically said whatever they had to say, which, in most cases, was probably not much.

ALGERNON   I'll speak to Bunbury, Aunt Augusta, if he is still conscious, and I think I can promise you he'll be all right by Saturday. Of course the music is a great difficulty. You see, if one plays good music, people don't listen, and if one plays bad music, people don't talk. But I'll run over the programme I've drawn out, if you will kindly come into the next room for a moment.

LADY BRACKNELL   Thank you, Algernon. It is very thoughtful of you. (*Rising, and following ALGERNON.*) I'm sure the programme will be delightful, after a few expurgations. French songs I cannot possibly allow. People always seem to think that they are improper, and either look shocked, which is vulgar, or laugh, which is worse. But German sounds a thoroughly respectable language, and indeed, I believe is so. Gwendolen, you will accompany me.

GWENDOLEN   Certainly, mamma. (*LADY BRACKNELL and ALGERNON go into the music-room. GWENDOLEN remains behind.*)

The Importance of Being Earnest Oscar Wilde

Comprehension

1 In the extract from the play, Lane is the butler and Jack is a friend of Algernon. Sort out the other relationships between the characters.   (2)

2 What do we learn from the passage of Lady Bracknell's attitude towards
  a) Jack
  b) Gwendolen
  c) her husband?   (6)

3 What is the implication in Lane's answer, 'No, sir. Not even for ready money'? (2)

4 What is the point of the remarks about Lady Harbury? (2)

5 What is implied by the stage direction in line 46? (2)

6 What can you deduce from the passage about Mr Bunbury? (4)

7 What is the attitude of
   a) Gwendolen
   b) Algernon
   towards Lady Bracknell? (4)

8 Write a short account of a time when you were caught out giving a false excuse. (8)

Total (30)

A Boy and Two Girls

After we had waited for ten minutes in the crowded tea shop, the clergy-man's son came lumbering through the door. My heart leapt and I could feel myself growing pale, my knees under the gingham tablecloth began to tremble. 'There he is,' I whispered.

5 'Where?'

'There, by the door.'

'You mustn't *wave* to him like that! He'll think you want to see him!'

'Well, I do want to see him!'

'Hush, here he comes.'

10 'I say, isn't he *tall* . . .' She moved up on the oak pew, making room for him.

'Hullo,' I said.

'Hullo,' he said.

We smiled at each other and he clapped his hands together, knocked

15 against a woman at the next table, apologised, at last fitted himself into the pew with his back to Ireen.

'This is Ireen,' I said.

He swivelled round, pulling the tablecloth with him. There was demerara sugar all over the place. He slapped about with a rather dirty handkerchief

20 and Ireen said it didn't matter at all. He then said, 'How do you do?' and held out his big hand which grew out of his rather skimpy sleeve like a beautiful cabbage. She shook it delicately. He then sat on his hands, as though to prevent further damage.

'I've heard so much about you,' Ireen said. Her eyelids were fluttering as

25 mine did when I was trying not to cry. I thought perhaps she had hurt herself in the scuffle. 'It's so nice to meet you at last.'

'Well,' he said. But nothing came after. He was staring at her. Her eyelids beat up and down and for some reason she had clenched the tip of her tongue between her teeth and was smiling at the same time. This gave her

30 the look of a complete maniac. At least two whole minutes went by, while I held my breath and wondered what on earth was happening. Was she

having a fit? Was this normal? Should I scream or faint or simply carry on with the conversation?

'Are you going to have an ice-cream?' I said.

35 'No. No. I can't stop. I can't stay. I've got to . . .'

'Oh, but you *must*!' Ireen said, and put her hand on his arm, at the same time impossibly moving her body at least six inches towards him. 'You simply *must* stay.'

Now I knew that in daylight, in public places, the clergyman's son was
40 untouchable. To brush against him by accident was enough to send him crashing away, hair tossing, arms flailing, a fearful embodiment of terror and disgust. Therefore when Ireen assaulted him, so to speak, I drew in my breath, knowing what would happen. He leapt up as though shot, took two steps backwards and overturned a hatstand, whirled round and hit a small
45 child over the head with his great uncontrollable hand, bent sideways, grabbed the hatstand, looked desperately at the screaming child, dropped the hatstand, leapt over the pile of fallen coats straight into a waitress with a tray, turned, gasped, gave a hunted cry and was gone. I let out my breath and took a mouthful of ice-cream. The café reassembled itself round me with
50 sounds of protest and distress.

'What a pity,' I said. 'He doesn't like you.'

'Doesn't *like* me?'

'You have to be very careful with some boys,' I said. 'You have to know how to deal with them.'

55 'If you think he ran away like that because he didn't *like* me – ' she shouted, outraged.

I licked my spoon, stroking my tongue with it. 'I know he did.'

The Pumpkin Eater Penelope Mortimer

Comprehension

1 What is there to suggest that the narrator was looking forward to meeting the boy?

2 How does her reaction differ from Ireen's when they see him?

3 Why did he swivel round?

4 Which word suggests the boy knew he was clumsy?

5 What did the narrator think was the reason why Ireen was fluttering her eyelids?

6 What do you think was the reason?

7 What caused the clergyman's son to react in the way he did?

8 What is the meaning of assault as used here and why did the writer add 'so to speak'?

9 What is the purpose of the final line?

10 Explain exactly the meaning and effect of the following words as used:
lumbering, pew, fearful embodiment, flailing.

11 Explain the following and say what they contribute to the description of the son:
a) like a beautiful cabbage
b) fitted himself into the pew

12 Write a short account of what the boy felt and thought, or describe what happened from the point of view of the waitress.

Pre-War Morocco

Most of Morocco is so desolate that no wild animal bigger than a hare can live on it. Huge areas which were once covered with forest have turned into a treeless waste where the soil is exactly like broken-up brick. Nevertheless, a good deal of it is cultivated, with frightful labour. Everything is done by
5   hand. Long lines of women, bent double, work their way slowly across the fields, tearing up the prickly weeds with their hands, and the peasant gathering lucerne for fodder pulls it up stalk by stalk instead of reaping it, thus saving an inch or two on each stalk. The plough is a wretched wooden thing, so frail that one can easily carry it on one's shoulder, and fitted underneath
10   with a rough iron spike which stirs the soil to a depth of about four inches. This is as much as the strength of the animals is equal to. It is usual to plough with a cow and a donkey yoked together. Two donkeys would not be quite strong enough, but on the other hand two cows would cost a little more to feed. The peasants possess no harrows; they merely plough the soil several
15   times over in different directions, finally leaving it in rough furrows, after which the whole field has to be shaped with hoes into small oblong patches to conserve water. Except for a day or two after the rare rainstorms there is never enough water. Along the edges of the fields channels are hacked out to a depth of thirty or forty feet to get at the tiny trickles which run
20   through the subsoil.

Every afternoon a file of very old women passes down the road outside my house, each carrying a load of firewood. All of them are mummified with age and the sun, and all of them are tiny. It seems to be generally the case in primitive communities that the women, when they get beyond a certain
25   age, shrink to the size of children. One day a poor old creature who could not have been more than four feet tall crept past me under a vast load of wood. I stopped her and put a five-sou piece (a little more than a farthing) into her hand. She answered with a shrill wail, almost a scream, which was partly gratitude but mainly surprise. I suppose that from her point of view,
30   by taking any notice of her, I seemed almost to be violating a law of nature. She accepted her status as an old woman, that is to say, as a beast of burden. When a family is travelling it is quite usual to see a father and a grown-up son riding ahead on donkeys, and an old woman following on foot, carrying the baggage.

35   But what is strange about these people is their invisibility. For several weeks, always at about the same time of day, the file of tiny old women had hobbled past the house with their firewood, and though they had registered themselves on my eyeballs I cannot truly say that I had seen them. Firewood was passing – that was how I saw it. It was only that one day I happened
40   to be walking behind them, and the curious up-and-down motion of a load of wood drew my attention to the human being beneath it. Then for the first time I noticed the poor old earth-coloured bodies, bodies reduced to bones and leathery skin, bent double under the crushing weight. Yet I suppose I had not been five minutes on Moroccan soil before I noticed the overloading

45 of the donkeys and was infuriated by it. There is no question that the donkeys are damnably treated. The Moroccan donkey is hardly bigger than a St Bernard dog; it carries a load which in the British Army would be considered too much for a large mule, and very often its pack-saddle is not taken off its back for weeks together. But what is peculiarly pitiful is that

50 it is the most willing creature on earth: it follows its master like a dog and does not need either bridle or halter. After a dozen years of devoted work it suddenly drops dead, whereupon its master tips it into the ditch and the village dogs have torn its guts out before it is cold.

This kind of thing makes one's blood boil, whereas – on the whole – the

55 plight of the human being does not. Moroccan peasants are next door to invisible. Anyone can be sorry for the donkey with its chafed back, but it is generally owing to some kind of accident if one even notices the patient old woman under her load of sticks.

Marrakesh George Orwell

Comprehension

1 The first paragraph deals with the (14) cultivation of land in Morocco. Quote seven of the details in the paragraph which describe how this cultivation is carried out, and after each detail explain how it helps to demonstrate the poverty of those who are doing the work and the poor conditions under which they work. Begin a new line for each detail.

2 Using your own words as far as (10) possible, describe the appearance, way of life and attitudes of old women in Morocco, as suggested in the second paragraph.

3 Compare and contrast each of the (12) author's reactions and attitudes to Moroccan donkeys with his reactions and attitudes to old women, as suggested in the third and fourth paragraphs. Justify each point you make by a brief reference to the passage.

4 For each of the following statements write *True* or *False*, and then give a reason for your choice, based on the passage.
a) The author is Moroccan by birth.
b) A mule, according to the author, is stronger than a donkey.
c) There is no natural source of irrigation in Morocco other than rainwater.
d) Not all the food grown by Moroccan peasants is for human consumption. (8)

5 In what way does a fact mentioned in (4) the first paragraph make the occupation of the old women, described in paragraphs two and four, surprising?

6 Explain briefly the meaning of each of the following words as used in the passage:
a) primitive (line 24)
b) violating (line 30)
c) plight (line 55)
d) chafed (line 56) (4)

Total (52)
JMB *Paper B*

Examiners' comments

Orwell's passage was perhaps too deeply personal to communicate all its subtleties of feeling to candidates sitting an examination. Although some were able to cope quite well with the demonstrations of poverty in question (1) and with the physical appearance and philosophy of the old women in question (2), the technique for answering question (3) eluded very many. Yet this was the question central to the passage. Too few candidates were able to pick out Orwell's immediate anger at the plight of the donkeys and contrast it with his lack of sympathy on first seeing the old women under their back-breaking bundles of firewood. Only the best candidates were able to see an eventual admiration for both the 'willing' donkeys and the 'patient' old women. Most serious of all was the refusal of numerous candidates to point out the author's attitude, preferring instead to refer to the attitude of people in general or to invent attitudes not even implied in the text.

Question (4), a type common on this paper, was handled competently, although surprisingly few candidates scored full marks. Question (5) evoked many inaccurate guesses, candidates not having read the passage closely enough to be puzzled about how a 'treeless waste' produced bundles of firewood. Question (6) was answered rather better than its equivalent in recent years, the main problem being 'chafed', with its implication of 'rubbed'. A number of candidates hazarded the guess that it meant 'hollowed out'.

A Woman Challenging the Arctic

As I approached the Grand Banks it became bitterly cold. It was as if the wind had blown out of an enormous refrigerator, and I could almost feel the arctic ice in its breath. There was a different smell in the air too, a strong scent of fish and decaying sea life, carried down with melting ice.

5 And, as always, there was fog. Sometimes it would fade a little, but then it would swoop down thick as ever, and we would be sailing into a white curtain again. I tried not to peer ahead too often because all I could see were the hundreds of icebergs my eyes conjured up and my nerves could not stand the strain.

10 The place had a terrible emptiness to it, a desolation that entered one's bones with every blast of icy wind. I had a strong impression of space and distance and for once I was aware of how very far from land we were. Normally I never thought beyond the three miles of water I could see around me, a miniature world across which the *Golly* seemed to be sailing forever.

15 But here, I was aware of what I was, a small person in the middle of a large ocean. And it was a cold and lonely feeling.

Loneliness was not something I often experienced at sea. I missed people, which is an entirely different thing, for it holds the promise of reunion and renewed companionship in the future. Also, the boat and the sea themselves

20 were familiar old friends and, until either gave me cause to believe otherwise, I felt safe in their company. I have only ever felt real loneliness in big cities or other places where there are plenty of people about but no one to talk to. Normally I dislike being alone and if there are people around I will always seek them out. But here there was not much chance of finding

25 someone to talk to so I didn't feel I was missing anything. It was the difference of going for a walk on your own with the prospect of seeing the family for tea and coming home to a silent and empty house to find a note stuck on the door: 'Gone to a party – you're invited too!' but no indication as to where the party might be.

30 Out here in the deathly quiet and dank fog, I suddenly wanted to be where I was sure everybody else must be: in the warm and sunny ocean to the south. For a moment I even imagined that I had been sucked hundreds of miles to the north, and it was only by frequent looks at the compass and chart that I convinced myself I was indeed south of Newfoundland.

35 The best remedy for loneliness and thoughts of the Arctic was to keep myself occupied, but even when busy down in the cabin I felt an eerie atmosphere that made me shiver. Not that I wasn't shivering, anyway. However many clothes I put on I was still cold. I must have looked like an overweight teddy bear, and I certainly felt it as I rolled round the boat,

40 bouncing off the bulkheads. I wore so many layers that my arms stuck out from my sides as if my deodorant had turned to concrete. On top of a vest and paper panties I wore Mother's thermo-nuclear underwear consisting of silky long johns and top, then a polar suit made of thick tufted wool, and finally a pair of old jeans and two very baggy sweaters. On my head I wore

45 a wool balaclava and around my neck a towel. When going on deck I would put oilskin on top of all this, although it was a tremendous effort to haul them on and resulted in much puffing and panting. However, after I had been sail changing or winching for a while I would regret nearly every layer of clothing. Within minutes I would be dying of heat, and inside my super
50 efficient oilskin it felt like the hothouse at Kew; very warm, very humid and very uncomfortable.

But while my body was burning hot, my hands were freezing. The one thing I had forgotten was gloves. Not that I could have worn them to handle the ropes, but it would have been nice to keep my hands warm between sail
55 changes so that they couldn't freeze so quickly on deck.

Come Hell or High Water Clare Francis

Comprehension

1 For each of the following statements write *True* or *False* and then give a reason for your choice based on what is stated or suggested in the passage.
  a) Clare Francis likes to be on her own.
  b) There were hundreds of icebergs around her in the fog.
  c) She is a well-organised person.
  d) In this part of the journey she is travelling towards the Arctic. (8)

2 Describe the physical discomforts and mental pressures that she experienced and say how she attempted to counteract them. (12)

3 Although in line 6 she says *we*, she is on her own.
  a) Why do you think she says *we*?
  b) What is there to indicate that she is on her own? (4)

4 Explain the distinction she makes in paragraph 4 between loneliness and not being with people. (4)

5 How practical were the clothes that she wore? (4)

6 What indications are there that sailing a boat under these conditions was very strenuous? (2)

7 Write 10 to 15 lines on *one* of the following:
  a) What qualities do you think are needed to attempt what Clare Francis did, that is, sail round the world on her own? *or*
  b) Give a brief account of the different types of loneliness that people can experience. (12)

8 Explain how the following words or phrases are used in the passage: (8)
  a desolation that entered one's bones (line 10)
  deathly quiet (line 30)
  dank fog (line 30)
  a miniature world (line 14)

9 Do you find it odd that in spite of the conditions she used a deodorant? Give reasons for your answer. (2)

Total (56)

Further work

10 Fill in the blanks in the following sentences with either his or her:

   a) The bad-tempered driver damaged _____ car.

   b) _____ loving care for the old people was recognised by all.

   c) The criminal was caught trying to escape from _____ home.

   d) The miser did not trust banks, but kept _____ money under the bed.

   e) A good parent looks after _____ children carefully.

   Consider your answers carefully.

   Which qualities and situations have you associated with men and which with women?

   Why do you think this is so?

Topics for dicussion

1 What Clare Francis did was brave, but especially brave for a woman.

2 She would have contributed more to human happiness by devoting her energies to the sick.

3 When a woman does a job normally associated with a man more is expected of her than of the man.

4 Women should not be expected to do heavy work such as road digging or coal mining.

5 When there is high unemployment men with families should have priority over married women for jobs.

6 Women do not have their fair share of well-paid jobs.

7 Both boys and girls should do woodwork, needlework and cookery at school.

8 What occupations, jobs, household duties, do you associate with men and women. How justified is the division?

9 Most newspapers have a Woman's Page. Do you think this is justified?

10 Are there magazines, TV programmes, etc. that appeal more to women than to men, and vice versa?

Research

Use the library and reference books to find out facts about the following:

The achievements of individual women.

The number of women MPs and their places in Parliament.

The part played by women in Trade Unions, noting particularly the number of women in top Union posts.

The Trout

George and I, and the dog, left to ourselves, went for a walk to Wallingford on the second evening, and, coming home, we called at a little river-side inn, for a rest.

We went into the parlour and sat down. There was an old fellow there,
5   smoking a long clay pipe, and we naturally began chatting.

He told us that it had been a fine day to-day, and we told him that it had been a fine day yesterday, and then we all told each other that we thought it would be a fine day to-morrow; and George said the crops seemed to be coming up nicely.

10   After that it came out, somehow or other, that we were strangers in the neighbourhood, and that we were going away the next morning.

Then a pause ensued in the conversation, during which our eyes wandered round the room. They finally rested upon a dusty old glass-case, fixed very high up above the chimney-piece, and containing a trout. It rather fascinated
15   me, that trout; it was such a monstrous fish. In fact, at first glance, I thought it was a cod.

'Ah!' said the old gentleman, following the direction of my gaze, 'fine fellow that, ain't he?'

'Quite uncommon,' I murmured; and George asked the old man how
20   much he thought it weighed.

'Eighteen pounds six ounces,' said our friend, rising and taking down his coat. 'Yes,' he continued, 'it wur sixteen year ago, come the third o'next month, that I landed him. I caught him just below the bridge with a minnow. They told me he wur in the river, and I said I'd have him, and so I did. You
25   don't see many fish that size about here now, I'm thinking. Good night, gentlemen, good night.'

And he went out, and left us alone.

We could not take our eyes off the fish after that. It really was a remark-ably fine fish. We were still looking at it, when the local carrier, who had
30   just stopped at the inn, came to the door of the room, and he also looked at the fish.

'Good-sized trout, that,' said George, turning round to him.

'Ah! you may well say that, sir,' replied the man; and then he added, 'Maybe you wasn't here, sir, when that fish was caught?'
35   'No,' we told him. We were strangers in the neighbourhood.

'Ah!' said the carrier, 'then, of course, how should you? It was nearly five years ago that I caught that trout.'

'Oh! Was it you who caught it, then?' said I.

'Yes, sir,' replied the genial old fellow. 'I caught him just below the lock
40   – leastways, what was the lock then – one Friday afternoon; and the remark-able thing about it is that I caught him with a fly. I'd gone out pike fishing, bless you, never thinking of a trout, and when I saw that whopper on the end of my line, blest if it didn't take me quite aback. Well, you see, he weighed twenty-six pound. Good night, gentlemen, good night.'
45   Five minutes afterwards, a third man came in, and described how he had

caught it early one morning, with bleak*; and then he left, and a stolid, solemn-looking, middle-aged individual came in, and sat down over by the window.

None of us spoke for a while; but, at length, George turned to the
50 newcomer, and said:

'I beg your pardon, I hope you will forgive the liberty that we – perfect strangers in the neighbourhood – are taking, but my friend here and myself would be so much obliged if you would tell us how you caught that trout up there.'

55 'Why, who told you I caught that trout?' was the surprised query.

We said that nobody had told us so, but somehow or other we felt instinctively that it was he who had done it.

'Well, it's a most remarkable thing – most remarkable,' answered the stranger, laughing; 'because, as a matter of fact, you are quite right. I did
60 catch it. But fancy your guessing it like that. Dear me, it's really a most remarkable thing.'

And then he went on, and told us how it had taken him half an hour to land it, and how it had broken his rod. He said he had weighed it carefully when he reached home, and it had turned the scale at thirty-four pounds.

65 He went in his turn, and when he was gone, the landlord came in to us. We told him the various histories we had heard about his trout, and he was immensely amused, and we all laughed very heartily.

'Fancy Jim Bates and Joe Muggles and Mr Jones and old Billy Maunders all telling you that they had caught it. Ha! ha! ha! Well, that is good,' said
70 the honest old fellow, laughing heartily. 'Yes, they are the sort to give it to me to put up in my parlour, if they had caught it, they are! Ha! ha! ha!'

And then he told us the real history of the fish. It seemed that he had caught it himself, years ago, when he was quite a lad; not by any art or skill, but by that unaccountable luck that appears to wait always upon a boy when
75 he plays the wag from school, and goes out fishing on a sunny afternoon, with a bit of string tied on to the end of a tree.

He said that bringing home that trout had saved him from a whacking, and that even his schoolmaster had said it was worth the rule of three and practice put together.

80 He was called out of the room at this point, and George and I again turned our gaze upon the fish.

It really was a most astonishing trout. The more we looked at it, the more we marvelled at it.

It excited George so much that he climbed up on the back of a chair to
85 get a better view of it.

And then the chair slipped, and George clutched wildly at the trout-case to save himself, and down it came with a crash, George and the chair on top of it.

'You haven't injured the fish, have you?' I cried in alarm, rushing up.

* small fish used as bait

90   'I hope not,' said George, rising cautiously and looking about.

But he had. That trout lay shattered into a thousand fragments – I say a thousand, but they may have been only nine hundred. I did not count them.

We thought it strange and unaccountable that a stuffed trout should break up into little pieces like that.

95   And so it would have been strange and unaccountable, if it had been a stuffed trout, but it was not.

That trout was plaster of Paris.

Three Men in a Boat Jerome K Jerome

Comprehension

1 Why did George and the author repeat that they were strangers? (2)

2 Compare the four accounts of the way the trout was caught. Pay attention to the different points of fact, e.g. the size of the trout and also to the way the subject was brought up. (12)

3 What is there to suggest that there was a conspiracy among the four men? (4)

4 Why were George and the author so easily deceived at first? (2)

5 At what point are we made aware that they realised they were being fooled? (2)

6 How does the author achieve a humorous climax to the incident? (8)

Total (30)

Children in Factories

In 1832 John Doherty published the *Memoir of Robert Blincoe*, a description of what mill life had been like at the turn of the century, by a boy who had been 'apprenticed' out of a London workhouse to a northern cotton mill. It was a horrifying tale of ill-usage. The children had had to adapt their
5 actions to the pace of the machines: any boy who was too slow, and held things up, was savagely beaten. Accidents were common; and when one of Blincoe's fingers got crushed in a machine, he was not allowed to stop working. If the children's hair grew verminous, it was treated by pitch-capping – a technique in common use at the time by forces in Ireland, as
10 a means of intimidating rebels: hot pitch was put on the scalp, allowed to set, and then jerked off, removing the lice with the hair. On one occasion a *sadistic* overseer had hung Blincoe above a machine so that he had to lift his leg, to avoid losing it, every time the machine turned. Although the shift of mills to factory towns, and the diminishing use of *pauper* apprentices, had
15 changed conditions in the mills, there was enough evidence of ill-usage and brutality for people to wonder whether there might not still be Blincoes suffering in silence.

In mills, the working day was from twelve to twelve and a half hours 'while in several districts they are not less than thirteen'; and there were various
20 excuses which employers could use to make the children work still longer. Where a shorter day was worked by agreement on Saturday, the hours lost might have to be made up during the week. To regain time lost by stoppages – through the breaking of machinery, say, or inadequate water power during a drought – it was the custom 'to work sometimes half an hour, at other
25 times an hour, and occasionally even as much as two hours daily, until the whole of the lost time be made up'. When the children did not have to clean the machinery during their meal-breaks they had to clean it out of their working hours. And when local custom dictated that a day should be observed as a holiday, the adult workers were given the option of making
30 up the time, or having the pay deducted from their wages; 'generally they chose the former'. The children, in such circumstances, were not consulted. They had to work the longer hours, too.

The provisions of earlier Factory Acts had simply been disregarded. In any case, they applied only to cotton mills; and in other factories, hours and
35 conditions of work for children were at the *whim* of the owner, or his manager. 'We have forty-five children', the overseer of a Nottingham factory had told one of the investigators. 'Our regular day is from six to seven. It should be an hour for dinner, but it is only half an hour. No time allowed for tea or breakfast; there used to be a quarter of an hour for breakfast; it
40 is altered now. We call it twelve hours a day. Overtime is paid for extra. When we're busy we work over-hours. Our present time is still half past nine (beginning at six). It has been so all winter, and since to this time. We have some very young ones, as young as eight.' In other cases, the children spoke for themselves: "Have worked here two years; I am now fourteen; work

45 sixteen hours and a half a day. I was badly, and asked to stop at eight one
night lately, and I was told if I went I must not come back."

On ill-treatment of factory children, too, evidence given to the Royal
Commission of 1833 confirmed previous evidence. The mill-owners had
denied that the strap was as freely used for disciplinary purposes as had been
50 suggested; but the Commission's investigators heard many stories of harsh
punishments: "When she was a child too little to put on her own clothes,
the overlooker used to beat her till she screamed again . . ." "Has often seen
the workers beat cruelly. Has seen the girls strapped; but the boys were beat
so that they fell to the floor in the course of the beating, with a rope with
55 four tails called a cat." "The other night a little girl came home cruelly
beaten; wished to go before a magistrate, but was advised not."

Such an existence, the Commissioners felt, could not but produce evil
effects. The long hours could seriously *impair* the children's health, sometimes leading to 'serious, permanent and incurable disease'. The children's
60 minds also suffered, as even where education was provided, they were too
fatigued to benefit from it. The children would not be so tired, the
Commissioners argued, if they did not have to endure the full adult working
day. With shorter hours, there would be no need to take the strap to them,
except for *flagrant* indiscipline. For example an overseer described how, very
65 often, at the end of the day, the children 'were nearly ready to faint; some
were asleep; some were only kept to work by being spoken to, or by a little
chastisement, to make them jump up.' With shorter hours too, they could
get out into the open before and after work; their twisted bodies would
unwind, their lungs fill with fresh air. They would be able to attend school,
70 without the state interfering.

The Government, therefore, passed a bill forbidding the employment in
factories of children under nine and restricted the working hours of children
to forty-eight a week; moreover children between the ages of fourteen and
eighteen would not be allowed to work more than sixty-nine hours a week.

Poverty and the Industrial Revolution Brian Inglis

Comprehension

1 What evidence is there in the passage (10)
that the children were brutally
treated?

2 What evidence is there in the passage (10)
that the children worked long hours
with little rest?

3 What bad effects did the children (5)
suffer as a result of the long hours?

4 What were the purposes of the Royal (6)
Commission's recommendations?

5 Explain your reaction to the (3)
Government's bill.

6 Explain what is normally meant by (3)
'apprenticed' and why the word has
been placed within inverted commas
in the passage.

7 Why does the author tell us in the (2)
first paragraph that pitch-capping was
a technique used in Ireland in order
to intimidate rebels?

8 What evidence is there in the third (4)
paragraph that hours and conditions
of work were at the whim of the
overseer of the Nottingham factory?

9 What evidence is there in the passage (5)
that the children were very young?

10 Use 2 of the following words in the (2)
passage in sentences which show that
you understand their meaning:
sadistic, pauper, whim, impair,
flagrant

Total (50)

Suggested marking scheme

1 whipped if could not keep pace with machines/made to work (10)
with injuries/removal of lice by hot pitch/hung over machine
so leg lifted/if ill had to continue or lose job/girl beaten
because she could not put on own clothes/boys beaten to
floor/with cat/beaten girl wanted to complain/beaten to stay
awake

2 Saturday hours made up/stoppage hours made up/cleaning of (10)
machinery/holiday hours made up/regular hours, 13/short
lunch/no tea/breakfast/compulsory overtime/e.g. $15\frac{1}{2}$ hour
day/child worked $16\frac{1}{2}$ hours/children very tired at end of day

3 poor health/ill for life/overtired/beaten/poor education (5)

4 stop tiredness/punishment would lessen/healthier/better (6)
education/employers and adults could fix own hours/without
state legislation

5 better but still must be tired/health suffer/poor education (3)

6 learn craft/bound to master for period/used as slave labour (3)

7 brings out that it is a horrible punishment/children treated as (2)
criminals

8 dinner hour cut/tea/breakfast removed/work $12\frac{1}{2}$ but paid for (4)
12 hours/long hours when busy

9 as young as eight/twelve-year-old working $16\frac{1}{2}$ hours/child too (5)
young to put on clothes/little girl came home beaten/children
under nine hours restricted

10 2 marks: 1 mark each (2)

Total (50)

The marking scheme is only a guide; for example, brutal treatment could be
long hours in question 1.

Jaws

Below, Hooper waited until the bubbly froth of his descent had dissipated. There was water in his mask, so he tilted his head backward, pressed on the top of the faceplate, and blew through his nose until the mask was clear. He felt serene. It was the pervasive sense of freedom and ease that he always
5   felt when he dived. He was alone in blue silence speckled with shafts of sunlight that danced through the water. The only sounds were those he made breathing . . . a deep, hollow noise as he breathed in, a soft thudding of bubbles as he exhaled. He held his breath, and the silence was complete. Without weights, he was too buoyant, and he had to hold on to the bars to
10 keep his tank from clanging against the hatch overhead. He turned round and looked up at the hull of the boat, a grey body that sat above him, bouncing slowly. At first, the cage annoyed him. It confined him, restricted him, prevented him from enjoying the grace of underwater movement. But then he remembered why he was there, and he was grateful.

15   He looked for the fish. He knew it couldn't be sitting beneath the boat as Quint had thought. It could not 'sit' anywhere, could not rest or stay still. It had to move to survive.

     Even with the bright sunlight, the visibility in the murky water was poor . . . no more than forty feet. Hooper turned slowly around, trying to pierce
20 the edge of the gloom and grasp any sliver of colour or movement. He looked at his watch, calculating that if he controlled his breathing, he could stay down for at least half an hour more.

     He glanced downward, started to look away, then snapped his eyes down again. Rising at him from the darkling blue . . . slowly, smoothly . . . was
25 the shark. It rose with no apparent effort, an angel of death gliding towards an appointment foreordained.

     Hooper stared, enthralled, impelled to flee but unable to move. As the fish drew nearer, he marvelled at its colours: the flat brown-greys seen on the surface had vanished. The top of the immense body was a hard ferrous
30 grey, bluish where dappled with streaks of sun. Beneath the lateral line, all was dreamy, ghostly white.

     Hooper wanted to raise his camera, but his arm would not obey. In a minute, he said to himself, in a minute.

     The fish came closer, silent as a shadow, and Hooper drew back. The head
35 was only a few feet from the cage when the fish turned and began to pass before Hooper's eyes . . . casually, as if in proud display of its incalculable mass and power. The snout passed first, then the jaw, slack and smiling, armed with row upon row of serrate triangles. And then the black, fathomless eye, seemingly riveted upon him. The gills rippled . . . bloodless
40 wounds in the steely skin.

     Tentatively, Hooper stuck a hand through the bars and touched the flank. It felt cold and hard, not clammy but smooth as vinyl. He let his fingers caress the flesh . . . past the pectoral fins, the pelvic fin . . . until finally they were slapped away by the sweeping tail.

45   The fish moved off to the limit of Hooper's vision . . . a spectral silver-grey blur tracing a slow circle. Hooper raised his camera and pressed the trigger. He knew the film would be worthless unless the fish moved in once more, but he wanted to catch the beast as it emerged from the darkness.

    Through the viewfinder he saw the fish turn towards him. It moved fast,
50 tail thrusting vigorously, mouth opening and closing as if gasping for breath. Hooper raised his right hand to change the focus. Remember to change it again, he told himself when it turns.

    But the fish did not turn. A shiver travelled the whole length of its body as it closed on the cage. It struck the cage head on, the snout ramming
55 between two bars and spreading them. The snout hit Hooper in the chest and knocked him backward. The camera flew from his hands, and the mouthpiece shot from his mouth. The fish turned on its side, and the pounding tail forced the great body further into the cage. Hooper groped for his mouthpiece but couldn't find it. His chest was convulsed with the
60 need for air.

    The fish rammed through the space between the bars, spreading them still further with each thrust of its tail. Hooper, flattened against the back of the cage, saw the mouth reaching, straining for him. He remembered the power head, and he tried to lower his right arm and grab it. The fish thrust again,
65 and Hooper saw with the terror of doom that the mouth was going to reach him.

    The jaws closed around his torso. Hooper felt a terrible pressure as if his guts were compacted. He jabbed his fist into the black eye. The fish bit down, and the last thing Hooper saw before he died was the eye gazing at
70 him through a cloud of his own blood.

    The fish broke water fifteen feet from the boat, surging upward in a shower of spray. Hooper's body protruded from each side of the mouth, and as if in contempt and triumph, the fish hung suspended for an instant, challenging mortal vengeance.

Jaws Peter Benchley

Comprehension

1 How does the author give us the (2)
impression that Hooper is an
experienced diver (lines 1–17)?

2 Explain why, in the first
paragraph, Hooper is
a) annoyed by the diving cage; (1)
and yet
b) grateful for it. (2)

3 In your own words, describe the (3)
feelings which make diving
pleasurable for Hooper. Base your
answer on lines 1–14.

4 What evidence is there in the (2)
passage that Hooper had seen the
shark before?

5 Explain the meaning of the
following:
a) trying to pierce the edge of the
gloom (lines 19–20)
b) an appointment foreordained
(line 26)
c) row upon row of serrate
triangles (line 38)
d) a spectral silver-grey blur (lines
45–46)
e) challenging mortal vengeance
(lines 73–74) (5×2)

6 a) Why does Hooper not film the (2)
shark when it first approaches?
b) Why were his first camera shots (2)
(lines 46–7) likely to be worthless?
c) Why did Hooper change the (2)
camera's focus (line 51)?
d) Why did he anticipate having to (2)
change focus again?

7 Apart from the obvious terror in (5)
his final moments, what idea do
you get of Hooper's feelings about
the shark? Support your opinion
with evidence from the passage.

8 How does the author transform a (7)
large unintelligent fish into such an
impressive foe? (Consider the way
the creature is described/personified,
its actions, and the reactions of
others to it.) Support your views
with reference to the passage.

Total (40)

Further written work

1 Continue the passage with your own account
of the reactions to Hooper's death of the two
remaining men on the boat: Quint, a determined and experienced sea fisherman; and
Brody, the local police chief, who is a non-
swimmer.

2 In the story *Jaws*, the first shark attack
happens shortly before a public holiday
weekend when the beaches of the resort town
concerned would normally be crowded. Write
two contrasting descriptions: one picturing a
busy holiday weekend scene at the resort; the
other showing the resort unusually quiet once
the shark's presence has been publicised.

Oral work

3 Improvise a public meeting held in the tourist
resort Amity at the time of the shark's attacks,
called to debate whether or not to keep the
beaches open for the benefit of tourist trade on
which the town depends. Allocate the
following roles: indecisive mayor; a safety-
conscious police chief; concerned hoteliers and
shopkeepers; tour boat operators; Hooper's
parents; press reporters. Develop other roles
of your own invention.

4 Why, in your opinion, was the book/film *Jaws*
such a success?

5 Gather as much information as you can about
different types of shark and their habits.
Prepare a short talk (or a display of material).

Punctuation

Examiners comment that:

'Many otherwise satisfactory candidates made repeated errors in punctuation, and consequently had their score reduced. The most common punctuation error is the use of a comma where a stronger stop is needed.' (JMB)

'Many candidates had their marks reduced by their failure to punctuate correctly and, in particular, by substituting commas for full stops.' (AEB)

Punctuation marks are a feature of written English. In spoken English we have other means to express what we want to say. These include intonation, inflection, pause and emphasis. Some of these can be represented in written English by punctuation marks: e.g.

You are going on holiday?
You are going on holiday!
You are going on holiday.

Points to remember

1 Punctuation marks are part of the meaning: e.g.

Why did he run away? Because he was afraid?
Why did he run away? Because he was afraid.
Only the boys, who did not wear earrings, were allowed to play.
Only the boys who did not wear earrings were allowed to play.

2 Usage is changing, particularly the use of the comma. However, although usage is changing and there are many occasions where the use of the comma is optional, the inclusion of a comma nearly always alters, even if only slightly, the meaning: e.g.

Although she was deaf, she sang beautifully
Although she was deaf she sang beautifully
Even now, she still acts
Even now she still acts

3 Punctuation marks are signals, signals to:

a) **The grouping of words**
b) **Intonation and stress**

Mistakes in the groupings of words can produce the wrong sense groupings.

Exercises

1 The following short passage shows how misplaced, or omitted, punctuation marks can alter the meaning completely. It is obviously slightly exaggerated, but nevertheless it makes the point. Rewrite it correctly punctuated.

For half an hour the train remained stationary now thoroughly out of temper the man and his wife sat in the carriage vibrating their legs and buzzing softly. A number of flies tried to force their way through the windowpane exclaiming well be late for the picture. The dead man will start in a few minutes from now. The man started up and kicked in annoyance his wife. A meek little woman tried to pacify him with a sudden scream. The train started off again. Emitting clouds of black smoke and soot the man puffed his pipe impatiently while slobbering over the womans umbrella. The mans fat bull pup dozed and blinked. Twitching her ears to and fro the woman smiled hopefully climbing on to the mans lap. The bull pup was settling down to sleep when the train stopped again.

2 Rewrite the following sentences by using different punctuation marks so that the sentences have a different meaning. Do not change the word order.

a) Betty asked Bill Jones where are you going
b) The holiday cost £50 more than I expected
c) Charles II smiled one minute after he was executed
d) I enjoyed Macbeth but I did not like Macbeth
e) They knocked down the Duke of York to build a Motorway
f) Are women still not allowed to enter the church

How punctuation works

Rather than learn rules (and there are very few rules of punctuation that are not regularly broken by accomplished writers) it is better to decide what you want to say and then see what punctuation marks are available to help you do so.

The problem with a list of rules is that usage is constantly changing and the rules can become downright misleading. For example, in many books on English you will read that a comma indicates a short pause, and a full stop a longer pause. But consider the following sentences:

'Friends, and I think I may call you friends, you are mistaken in this. I will, therefore, overlook it.'

You would probably find that in actual speech there would be a longer pause at the first comma than at the first full stop. Likewise you will read that a full stop is used at the end of a sentence, but the following punctuation is not at all uncommon in modern English:

I went into the room slowly and fearfully. Silence everywhere. Not the slightest sound, not the slightest movement. And darkness everywhere.

However, as with most skills, it is better to learn good usage first and then how to develop variations.

Remember: **punctuation marks are signals to:**
Grouping of words
Intonation and Emphasis

Signals to groupings of words

This includes marking off sense groups and marking off interruptions. However, as punctuation marks are written or printed signals, you should also consider here typographical conventions such as indenting, paragraphing, leaving space, italics, and underlining.

Marking off sense groups

Punctuation marks control the flow of the meaning.

Full stop

The name indicates its function. When you want the flow of meaning to stop (as distinct from a long pause for emphasis) then use a full stop. A general rule is: once a sentence is completed grammatically then use a full stop. As stated above it is not unusual to find in modern English a full stop used before the sentence is completed grammatically. This is done in order to isolate each sense unit to achieve a particular effect. The use, however, of a comma where there should be full stop is frowned upon by the examiners.

Always think in terms of: Full Stop + Space + Capital Letter

Examples:
1 As he walked over to the window, he saw a light under the door. This surprised him.
2 We went abroad last year. However, this year we will stay at home.
3 Shakespeare lived in Stratford at the beginning and end of his life. Most of the time between was spent in London.

Exercises

Write out the following with the appropriate full stops and capital letters:

1 we stayed in London for two weeks it was very hot then but not too hot

2 the batsman scored slowly he was obviously out of practice the crowd became very impatient

3 mrs bennett is the silliest person in the book I would say mr collins was the most conceited

Colon

As a colon connects rather than separates it is weaker than a full stop but stronger than a comma. It may be used as follows:

1 to connect sentences or clauses that contrast sharply. e.g.
   Man proposes: God disposes.
2 to connect ideas or statements which are an extension or comment on the immediately previous statement. e.g.
   Punctuation is not something you add to writing: it is an inescapable part of writing.
3 to introduce a list. e.g.
   The word may be used as follows: as a verb, as a noun, or as an adjective.
4 to introduce direct speech when there is no verb of saying. e.g.
   His words were brief and to the point: 'Get out!'

Note that in 1 and 2 above a full stop would be acceptable, but a comma would be regarded as too weak.

Exercises

Punctuate the following by using a colon where appropriate.

1 United are well supported City have lower attendances.

2 The ingredients are as follows 10 eggs milk and 1 kilo of sugar.

3 I would explain it this way if you connect green with blue you will kill yourself.

4 Written above the doors was abandon hope all that enter here.

5 A long prison sentence is more than a punishment it completely destroys some men.

Semi-colon

This sign was introduced a long time after the colon had been in use. It can both separate and join parts of a sentence. When it separates it can be replaced by a comma; when it joins it can be replaced by a full stop. Its main functions are:

1 to draw together a number of short sentences on the same topic. e.g.
   The wind howled; the rain lashed down; the doors shook; even the window frames seemed insecure.

Full stops would be acceptable in the above sentence, but they would separate each sentence into an individual unit.

2 to separate items in a list of phrases or clauses. e.g.
   The town centre displayed a myriad of colours: brilliant red on the illuminated names; silver on the shop fronts; a deep gold coming from the interior of the shops; and the lights coming from the cars' reflection on the wet road.

Note: when the following connecting words introduce a new statement either a semi-colon or a full stop should be used before them; a comma will generally be insufficient:

also, moreover, nevertheless, however, hence, therefore, then. e.g.

She was a very confident woman; moreover, her confidence was well-founded.

It was a very difficult time; however, you know that better than I do.

The semi-colon is a most useful mark as its function ranges from a weak full stop to a strong comma.

Exercises

Use semi-colons in the following:

1 The house was full of tables two in the entrance four in the dining room six of different sizes in the living room and in the kitchen two more.

2 He crawled under the barbed-wire his chin tucked into his chest his elbows kept well down all of the equipment on the ground beside him.

3 Shortly afterwards he felt ill his face went red his temperature rose he could not focus his eyes he then collapsed.

4 He refused to join the Army yet he was not a coward.

5 Flowers and blossoms white gowns and frothy veils little girls in gorgeous dresses parents anxious that they are correctly dressed these are what I associate with a wedding.

6 She disliked coffee nevertheless she drank some out of politeness.

7 Frost coated the pavements ice hung from the gutters even the pond had frozen over.

8 The centre of the plate was intricately patterned its rim was blue the reverse side was a pale cream.

9 I did not see the concert on television however I did listen to it.

10 The woman fastened her coat she adjusted her hat she picked up her gloves then she left the house.

Single comma

There is a greater variety in the use of single commas than in any other punctuation mark. The modern tendency is to leave them out when their omission does not alter or obscure the meaning.

Remember: **commas are used inside sentences and are not adequate replacements for full stops or colons.**

Their main usages are:

1 to mark off items in a list. e.g.
I found two pens, a pencil, string, a knife, five toy soldiers and an electronic game in his pocket.
It is not usual to use a comma if 'and' joins the last two items.

2 to mark off words in a series. e.g.
The road was narrow, dark, uninviting, even dangerous.

3 to mark off a phrase or clause from the rest of the sentence. e.g.
Standing still in the middle of the road, the dog waited for the cars to pass.
Whenever I see an electronic game, I have to close my eyes.

(**Note** that in such sentences if the main statement comes first it is not unusual to omit the comma. e.g. I have to close my eyes whenever I see an electronic game.)
However ill you are, you must attend.

4 to separate sentences joined by a conjunction. e.g.
She was very tired, but she still carried on.
(Think in terms of *Comma* + BUT)

5 to separate the names or titles of people spoken to from what is said. e.g.
Susan, where are you going?
Why do you say that, Bill?
You, come here.
Dear Sir,

6 to avoid ambiguity. e.g.
John painted the door, and his father paid him for it.
How would you tend to read the above sentence if there was no comma?

7 to separate words actually spoken from verbs of saying. e.g.
He said, 'You may go now.'
'You may now go,' he said.

Note the punctuation when the verb of saying interrupts the direct speech. One: if it interrupts a sentence then it is usual to use a comma at the end of the first portion of direct speech and at the beginning of the next. e.g.

'I am going to London next week.'
'I am going to London,' he said, 'next week.'
'If you do go,' she replied, 'will you visit my brother?'

(**Note** the small 'w' in will.)

Two: if the interruption comes between two sentences then a comma is used at the end of the first portion, and a full stop after the verb of saying. The second portion of direct speech begins with a capital letter. e.g.

'I am going to London next week. The following week I shall be in Birmingham.'

becomes

'I am going to London next week,' he said. 'The following week I shall be in Birmingham.'

Exercises

Punctuate the following:

1 You must come home Bill his mother said.

2 No he replied it is too late now.

3 You can lead a horse to water but you cannot make him drink.

4 We work Saturdays and Sundays and get paid on Monday.

5 The dress was half-price but I had no money left.

Typographical aids

Note that spacing helps to mark off sense groups.

1 *Indentation for paragraphs* (cf., pp. 127) *and sub-paragraphs*
The margin helps the eye to see how the writing is broken up into sense groups.

2 *Leaving a space*
This is usual after a full stop, question mark, exclamation mark, colon or semi-colon. Think in terms of **full stop** + **space** + **capital letter**.

3 *Italics*
Often used in printing to separate the italicised words from the rest of the sentence.

4 *Underlining*
Used in the same way as italics.

Marking off interruptions

The point to note about this use of punctuation marks is that if you remove the interruption you do not alter the meaning or grammar of a statement. Try to be sparing in your use of any punctuation marks which indicate interruptions. Over-use of them can be confusing.

Brackets

These are the most obvious way of showing that a group of words is an interruption in a main flow of meaning. e.g.

England (and I mean England, not the British Isles) was invaded by Julius Caesar.

'When I first read "The Divine Comedy" (How is it a comedy?), I could not understand it.'

Note the capital H in How, the position of the question mark and of the comma.

If you take away the bracketed statements in both the above examples the rest still makes full sense.

Dashes

These perform the same function as brackets. Brackets are generally more distinctive. Do not use dashes in a sentence which contains a hyphen. e.g.

Fiona Fotheringay-Smith – the ill-behaved daughter of the mayor – was arrested last night.

Which are the dashes and which are the hyphens in this?

Pairs of commas

Note that in the following there must be a pair of commas, one comma at the beginning of the interruption and one at the end. Care must be taken in the placing of the second comma.

1 A straightforward interruption or insertion. e.g.
I am pretty sure, or I think I am, that we have seen this film before.

2 A pair of commas is used to mark off an explanatory interruption which has no connecting link with the word it is explaining. e.g.
Betty, the head prefect, introduced the speaker. My cousin, the one who went abroad, has just won an award.

These words are said to be *IN APPOSITION* to the noun. **Note** that the second comma is not needed if the words in apposition are at the end of the sentence. e.g.
I forgot to tell Mr Jones, the year tutor.

3 Study the two following sentences:
The men, who were six feet tall, joined the squad.
The men who were six feet tall joined the squad.

In the first sentence the pair of commas indicates an interruption, 'and they were six feet tall'. The interruption can be taken out without spoiling the meaning. The sentence tells us that it was men and not women that joined the squad.

In the second sentence, where there are no commas, the clause, 'who were six feet tall', is an essential part of the meaning and cannot be left out. It tells us the *type* of men who joined, i.e. men below six feet in height did not join.

Exercises

Explain how the removal of the commas in each of the following sentences alters the meaning:

1 All the passengers, who were injured, received treatment.

2 The house, which stands at the top of the hill, will be used for the TV series.

3 The boat, which came in first, was to be sold.

Inverted commas – quotation marks – speech marks

These mark off a special type of interruption.

1 To indicate the words actually spoken, i.e. direct speech. e.g.
'I am tired,' he yelled, 'of having to shout at you.'

Note:
a) that if the words spoken are a question or exclamation then ? or ! is used inside the inverted commas. e.g.
'Have you seen this film?' he asked.
b) that if the verb of saying is in the question form the ? comes outside the quotation marks. e.g.
Did he say, 'If you do that I will kill you'?
c) that a single set or double set of inverted commas is acceptable provided you are consistent. If you have to use inverted commas inside inverted commas start and finish with one type and use the other within it. e.g.
'Did you see "King Kong" on television last night?' or
"Did you see 'King Kong' on television last night?"

2 To mark off quotations, either a single word or passage. e.g.
You have used 'too' where you should have used 'to'.

3 To mark off the title of books, plays, records, the names of ships or pubs. Again special attention is being drawn to the names. e.g.
Rebecca does not appear in 'Rebecca'.
We are studying 'Twelfth Night'.
Is "Sky Space High" top of the charts?
The church is opposite 'The Dog and Partridge'.

Note: That in print, italics or underlining are sometimes used instead of the quotation marks; that the main words of the title start with capital letters.

Signals to intonation or emphasis

These punctuation marks help you to use the proper intonation or emphasis. They come at the end of the sentence or exclamation (in Spanish they are more helpfully placed at the beginning and end of a sentence).

Question mark

This is used only when the actual words of the question are written. e.g.
'Are you coming to the party?' she asked.
But
She asked if you were coming to the party.

Exclamation mark

This is used to indicate that the words are said with some force or stress. e.g.
'No! No! No!'
This mark should be used sparingly.

Underlining

Underlining is sometimes used to indicate emphasis. e.g.
I mean you and not him.

To clarify meaning

Apostrophe

1 The principal use of the apostrophe is to show that a letter or letters have been left out. e.g.

I will = I'll   I have = I've   She is = She's
It is = It's   They did not = They didn't

Remember: **if an apostrophe is used with ITS then it is ALWAYS BEFORE THE 'S' – IT'S.**

2 The use of the apostrophe to show possession is really the same as the above, because some seven or eight hundred years ago we used to add "es" to the end of the word to show possession. e.g. the girles home
When the 'e' was eventually dropped an apostrophe was used to show that it had been left out.
the girles room = the girl's room
the boyes school = the boy's school
the girlses room = the girls' room

The rule therefore is quite simple:
a) **If the possessor does not end in 's' then add apostrophe 's':**

men	(*the men's room*)	boy	(*the boy's name*)
man	(*the man's room*)	cat	(*the cat's tail*)
lady	(*the lady's hat*)		

b) **Also, if the possessor ends in 's' just add an apostrophe:**
boys (a boys' hobby = a hobby of boys)
girls (the girls' school = the school of the girls)
cats (a cats' home = a home of cats)
ladies (the ladies' home = the home of ladies)

c) **If a person's name ends in "s", e.g. James, then either an apostrophe or an apostrophe +s is added.**
The general usage is that for short names an apostrophe s is added, but for long names only the apostrophe is added, e.g.

St James's Square
Keats's Poems
but *Archimedes' Principle*
However, it is common to see Keats' Poems.

d) **The apostrophe is also used for plurals of words or figures which do not normally have a plural form. e.g.**
We will have no if's or but's.
He writes his C's like 6's.

120

Hyphen

This is used:

1 to avoid ambiguity in such words as re-sign, ill-behaved, six-feet. e.g.
Has the manager resigned / re-signed?
Have you recovered / re-covered the chair?
The soldiers re-formed / reformed.

2 as a guide to pronunciation, when a prefix ending in a vowel is added to a word beginning with a vowel: e.g. co-opt (coopt), co-operative, re-employ.

3 to form compound words, generally adjectives. e.g. ice-cold, good-sized, green-fingers.
If the compound word becomes established as a word in its own right, the hyphen is generally omitted. e.g. head master, head-master, headmaster

4 when a prefix is added to a noun or adjective which begins with a capital letter. e.g. anti-Christian, pro-German, un-English

Abbreviations

A full stop is generally used to indicate that a word has been abbreviated. e.g. B.A., Hon. Sec., N.S.P.C.C.

There is a tendency to leave out the full stop if the abbreviation ends with the same letter as the abbreviated word. e.g. Doctor = Dr   Mister = Mr

There is also a tendency to leave out the full stops if the abbreviation becomes an established word. e.g. BBC, GPO, radar

Exercises

Answer the questions on the punctuation of the following sentences:

1 Hundreds of years ago, men believed the Earth to be the central body of the Universe, with the Sun, Moon, planets and stars moving round it once every day. The modern picture is very different. The Earth is known to be a planet moving round the Sun; the Sun itself is an ordinary star; and our own particular star-system, or galaxy, contains about 100,000 million stars of the same kind as ours.

  a) What is the difference in the use of two commas round 'Moon' and round 'or galaxy'?
  b) Why are semi-colons used in the third sentence?
  c) Would any other punctuation mark be acceptable instead of the semi-colons?

2 Tapioca roots, which are about a foot long, are harvested in November. When fresh they contain large quantities of prussic acid and are highly poisonous. But this breaks down when they are dried.

  a) What is the effect of the pair of commas in the first sentence?
  b) Should there be a full stop before But?
  c) If a comma was used before But what would be the different effect?

3 The silence was suddenly broken by the distant thunder that came rolling over the white roofs. It came – there could be no doubt now – from beyond the northern hills that had once been London's playground. From the buildings on either side, little avalanches of snow went swishing out into the wide street: then the silence returned.

a) What other marks could be used instead of the dashes?
b) Would commas be acceptable?
c) Suggest an alternative and acceptable punctuation of the last sentence.

4 Jack and I were mad with excitement we had never seen anything so thrilling in our lives

And then suddenly we realised that there were three animals in the running not two how it happened no one could say we were all so intent on the race so hoarsely shouting come on Colonel or Christobal or Woodman's Axe wins that we had not noticed a shape like a vast grey boulder rolling across the countryside towards the course.

It was Charley who first saw Ranji pound on to the course Oly smoke he groaned and at the same moment everyone else became aware of the amazing turn that had come to the race.

Ranji got excited he had broken into the course a hundred yards in front of the leading horses and lifting his trunk and letting out a defiant squeal he began to charge down towards the winning post.

The horsemen must have had wonderful control of their animals. We heard the great gasps of their gallant breath as they went by – like the roaring of big bellows it seemed – and the iron pounding of their hooves; saw the searing red of their distended nostrils; and then the shouting reached our ears from the finishing post. "Dead heat! Dead heat!"

a) Punctuate the first four paragraphs.
b) Explain why each punctuation mark is used in the final paragraph.

5 The following are incorrectly punctuated. Rewrite them with the correct punctuation.

a) As the girls' room was very untidy I told her off about it,
b) This means that the music is not boring to listen to, as you are, to all intents and purposes being told a story.
c) If Billy Jones hes the first one who came on wins ill eat my hat she said in a loud voice
d) The caretaker went to check the store cupboard, the washing up liquid was getting low, hed have to get some more toilet rolls, the light bulbs were running low
e) I always like to sing she said in the bath.
f) You yes you Smith what are you doing there looking for my homework and why should your homework book be in my desk you know that youre not allowed in during break.

g) Mohammed murad was rushed with police escort to cairos racecourse where bets were placed on his behalf but thousands of racegoers were shocked and complained about mohammeds presence for when he was set down tenderly in the stand he was in his coffin he had died the day before now egypts ministry of the interior have held inquiries into why the coffin was diverted from its course to the cemetery the four escorting policemen have said that they suddenly felt an irresistible power from inside the coffin, forcing them to take it to the racecourse there they felt impelled to bet on certain horses which the deceased would have backed and by some divine guidance these horses won

h) in a row of beds in weymouth hospital dorset are four children all from one family all admitted within six days and all with appendicitis first came six year old peggy woodward desperately ill and now recovering then victor seven peggys twin sister jean twelve was admitted yesterday

i) pink elephants a publican can understand but landlord bill glover suspected something fishy when one of his regulars told him ive just run over a shark in your car park for apart from anything else bills pub the spread eagle in norfolk street reading is a long way from the sea but he stopped laughing when the customer returned tugging a five ft dead shark bill said last night it must have fallen from a lorry the police were as baffled as I was and they were not very keen to take it as lost property now it seems I am stuck with the shark unless the owner comes to collect it

j) An unappreciative employer forces sluggish and immature man nearly 33 to find almost any job in the lovely lake district over payment for unimpressive talents might conjure up a flicker of interest in the toils of business whilst a longing for an away from it all existence if fulfilled could result in early senility single of course replies if any to box 504.

Produce interesting sentences to fit the following patterns of punctuation using one word for each line.

1 _____ _____ _____ _____ _____
_____ _____: _____ _____ _____;
_____ _____; _____ _____ _____
_____.

2 _____ _____s' _____ _____ _____
_____ _____ _____ _____'s _____.

3 _____ _____, _____ _____ _____
_____ _____, _____ _____.

4 _____ _____ _____ _____ _____
_____ _____, _____, _____, _____
_____ _____.

5 _____, _____ _____ _____ _____
_____, _____ _____ _____; _____ _____,
_____ _____, _____ _____ _____.

6 _____ _____ _____ _____ (_____,
_____ _____ _____) _____ _____
_____ _____.

7 _____ _____ _____ _____ _____
_____ _____; _____ _____ _____
_____ _____.

8 '_____? _____ _____ _____!' _____
_____, _____.

9 " '_____' _____ _____ _____,' "
_____ _____, "_____ _____ _____
_____.' "
_____ _____ _____ _____.'

10 _____ _____ _____ _____ _____
_____ _____ _____: _____ _____
_____ _____ _____ _____.

Essays

Although essay writing does not feature prominently in most people's lives, it is a worthwhile activity. Most of what we have to write in everyday life is concerned with facts, either the transmission or evaluation of facts. The essay or composition gives you a chance to develop your own ideas and opinions, and to explore different areas of your imagination. Writing a story, creating a character or atmosphere, can be a source of joy and give a sense of satisfaction at the achievement. The essay, then, gives you a chance to show your own writing ability. The examiners are also interested in the quality of your thinking, your ability to arrange your thoughts, or impressions, in a coherent order, and to express them in clear, efficient language. However, one problem must be faced. When we write anything we always have someone in mind as our audience and this should affect the manner and style in which we write (see Registers). Students know they are writing for the benefit of their teachers, and candidates know that they are writing for the benefit of the examiners.

Examiners have tried to overcome this by giving structured essays or essays in which role-play plays an important part.

Essay writing in general

Planning

1 Time spent in choosing carefully a title is not time wasted. There may be one or two titles which need special knowledge and if you do not have that special knowledge cross those titles out. It is quite common for candidates under the pressure of an examination to think that they cannot write on any of the topics given. However, most examiners provide a wide variety of topics and it is most unlikely that you will not have anything worthwhile to say on all of them.

2 Make certain you have sufficient material to use. Often a title may seem attractive at first but when you come to think about it you find that you have only one or two things to say. This can be particularly bad if you need special knowledge or facts in order to write an essay of acceptable length. e.g.

Is pop music over-commercialised?

You may have an opinion on this but you need detailed information to support it.

3 Once you have chosen a title make certain that you understand it fully.

4 Underline key words in the title and as you write make certain that you write with those words in mind.

5 Do not change the title to one you would have preferred. There is a great difference between
'Holidays Abroad,' and 'A Holiday Abroad'.
Every year the examiners complain that prepared essays are given in place of essays on a similar subject that the examiners have set.

6 If you are asked to write an essay or story using a picture as a guide or stimulus, make certain you do use it as such. Study the picture and jot down the main details in it. Then decide whether you are going to write a narrative, description or argument based on the picture.

7 It follows that some sort of plan is needed. This need not be elaborate but you should have some general idea of what the start, middle and finish of the essay are going to be.

The golden rules to remember in the preparation of an essay are:

1 Always think in terms of structure

A comparison with a house helps in this respect. The overall plan may be regarded as the general outline or outside view of the house; the paragraphs are the different rooms with their different contents and different functions; the sentences within the paragraphs are the items within the room.

2 Paragraphing is important

Although the paragraphs are the self-contained rooms in the house, each one needs a connecting door to the next. A good essay is a tour of the subject (house) and the tour goes progressively from one area to the next. A poor essay is a tour which misses out many of the rooms and, instead of progressing, keeps on returning to one or two rooms.

Paragraphing

All skills in English are developed only by constant practice. The more you write, the better your writing should become. Use the following as ideas for single paragraphs. Make certain that the paragraph relates only to the idea given, or an extension of it, or supporting arguments to it.

1 When younger pupils complain in school about being bullied by the older pupils, they often omit to tell important details.
2 The colours of autumn have a richness . . .
3 Boredom is often the cause of vandalism. Where I live . . .
4 The weather was even more miserable that day.

How essays are marked

There are two ways in which essays are marked in examinations:
1 by impression marking
2 by analytic marking.

Impression marking

The examiner reads the essay two or three times and then awards it a mark based on the general impression that the essay has given him.

Analytic marking

A set number of marks is awarded for different aspects of the essay. A typical analytic marking scheme is as follows:

Total marks available: 100
20 marks available for each of the following categories:
a) *subject matter* or content (20 marks)
   i.e. ideas, quality of the argument or description, depth or superficiality, relevance to the title.
b) *construction of the essay* (20 marks)
   i.e. development of ideas, satisfactory opening and conclusion, use of paragraphs to develop the topic.
c) *vocabulary and expression* (20 marks)
   i.e. appropriateness of vocabulary to the topic, range of vocabulary, sentence construction and variety of types of sentences, general style.
d) *mechanical accuracy* (20 marks)
   i.e. spelling, punctuation, grammatical accuracy, use of capital letters. This part of the marking scheme generally differs from the others in that for the other categories the examiners award marks, whereas in this category they start with the maximum marks and take off marks, or half-marks, for errors. When the total mark available has been used up then no more marks are deducted.
e) *general impression* (20 marks)
   The examiner often reads the essay again to see if he or she has been too harsh or generous, and gives a mark based on the general impression.

All 5 marks are then added up to form the mark awarded to the candidate for the essay.

Some Examination Boards double-mark essays, that is, the essay is marked by one examiner who gives it an impression mark, and then it is marked by a different examiner who uses an analytical marking scheme.

Grading of sample essays

The following are examples of essays written under examination conditions. The first (essay A), was regarded by the examiners as being worthy of Grade A, which is the highest grade. Essay B was regarded as an example of a Grade D, that is, just below what could be regarded as a pass standard. **Note** that Grade A does not mean that there are no mistakes in it, and a Grade D does not mean that it is totally without merit. Essays C to F that follow have not been graded yet.

1 If you are part of a group arrange for half of the group to give an impression mark for the first essay, and half of the group to give an analytical mark for the same essay.

2 Discuss the difference between:
   a) marks awarded by the different types of markers;
   b) widely different marks by the same type of markers.

3 Mark the remaining essays either by impression or by the analytical marking scheme. Note the effect the handwriting and general layout has on your attitude towards each essay and towards the mark you give.

A Holidays Abroad

<u>Holidays abroad</u>

Last year, all of our family, Mum, Dad, John, who is my younger brother, and I went to Spain for our holidays. It was the third year in succession that we had been abroad. The previous year we went to Majorca and before that to Italy. Our first holiday abroad was in Switzerland. I didn't enjoy that very much, but I have enjoyed all the others. Perhaps it was because I was older and able to find more things to enjoy. Unfortunately we cannot afford any sort of a holiday this year, that is except for a few days out. Dad was made redundant shortly after coming back from Spain and Mum has been on short time for nearly as long.

It is not that holidays abroad are all that expensive, unless of course you go for one of the fancy places like Hawaii or China. In fact Dad always says that if we went to a hotel in England with all the facilities we've had in the hotels abroad we would be charged the earth. We found that the cost of one week's holiday at a reasonable hotel (not a posh one!) at the seaside here was more than a fortnight's holiday in Spain — and that included the air fares.

One of the things I will miss is looking through the brochures. We used to get as many as we could in November and compare them all. And the family arguments they started! The year we went to Italy Mum wanted to go to Malta, Dad wanted to go to Majorca again and I wanted to go to the French Riviera. For two weeks there was Civil War in the house and then the Cold war set in. We eventually decided on Italy (Venice) as nobody was insisting on going there.

I love looking through the catalogues even after we have booked for a place. The only thing is that I can't stop the fancy language used in them coming into my head whenever I come across one of the names. 'Sun-kissed shores' 'white dazzling sands' 'gorgeous tans' these aren't just empty phrases for me — they are real. I love sunbathing and when you go abroad you can nearly always be sure of the sun. I also love the beach boats and being able to wear light dresses or shorts all the time. Every hotel we have stayed in has had a swimming pool with lovely chairs and umbrellas at the side.

Many people like to go abroad to find out about different scenes and customs. I'm not much one for sight seeing myself but it's always a change if you get fed up of lying on the beach. Before we went to Italy everyone kept telling us that the men went around pinching you on the bum. Dad said that he would clobber anyone that tried it and then in the next breath he told mum that she needn't worry as it would only be the blind or the short-sighted that would try it with her. He thought that very funny — Mum didn't.

The two things I am not all that mad about going abroad are flying and some of the food. My brother loves the flying, but I don't. I'm not as bad as Mum, though. She sits all through the flight clutching the arms of the seat, drinking brandy. She worries about a wing falling off and whether the pilot's too young or too old. I'm glad when we've landed safely. Some of the food I like but some I don't. We once had a massive plate of rice with fish in it but I'm sure the prawns were alive or at least they looked like it. (I prefer the ice cream abroad).

However, these are only minor matters. For me the sun and sea, meeting people the entertainments (not the bullfights) are all that matter and if I get a job when I've left school part of my wages are going straight into the bank as I can't wait until I get a chance to have another holiday abroad.

B An Important Interview

An Important Interview

I don't want to stay on at school after I am 16 so I've been applying for lots of jobs. The trouble is I'm not quite sure what I want to do so I've been applying for all types of jobs except factory jobs I want some sort of job that has decent prospects. so far I have had only one reply giving me an interview it was for a junior post in a advertising firm.

I liked the look of it and it seemed to have possibilities but I know nothing about the firm. As the careers officer always told us it would be fatal to go for an interview to a firm you know nothing about. I went to the careers library. I couldn't find out anything about the firm but I got a lot of information about careers in advertising, the more I found out the more I liked it. One of our careers hand outs told us to always make a list of questions that they might ask like why do you want to work for us and what are your hobbies so I did.

My father told me not to wear jeans or leather jacket (he works in a bank) but as I hadn't a suit I put my school uniform on. I thought this might impress them.

I wanted to make sure I got there on time but the bus was late and I had to run. I needent of as when I got there there were five others waiting for the same job.

After a while we all started talking and comparing schools. One girl had applied for more than 30 jobs and this was her fourth interview

She seemed very confident as did another lad who kept on telling us he had 8 o'levels. As the rest of us had not taken any yet we had to boast about other achievements.

I was third to be interviewed. When I went in I was shivering inside and my mouth was dry. There were two men sitting at a desk and a woman sitting at the side. All of them were casually dressed they didn't have ties and suits and the woman wore one of those one piece track suit things. I was asked to sit on a low chair in front of the desk. One of the men told me to relax and that it was all going to be friendly and chatty. He checked my name and address and I croaked out my reply but at least he got me talking and my mouth became less dry. The second man then said

'Now Mr. Barry tell us about yourself'

'What do you want to know' I said

'Whatever you think important'

So I told him my age, name, address, the school and what my hobbies were. All of a sudden the woman who was at side just behind me asked me have you got permission to have time off school to come for this interview. When I hesitated she said its obvious you haven't she then asked me how much salary do you think your worth? This threw me completely as I didn't know what the job was. Then I remembered that my sister Sue whose only just 18 gets £65 so I said £60. They all smiled when I said that. The first man then asked me what I know about advertising and as I didn't know alot I had to rabbit on a bit. The 2nd man said

'Why don't you admit that the only thing you know about it is what you see on the telly and in newspapers?'

Before I had time to admit he went on to tell me about the job and what my duties would be. I can't say I found it very interesting. The woman then said were do you expect to be in 10 years time? I just looked at her and said I don't know - Married I suppose.

They then asked me if I wanted to ask any questions. I had prepared a list of what I thought were sharp questions, but I was so nervous I forgot everyone and just asked them when would I start if I got the job. The first man said they would let me know within a few weeks and he stood up and thanked me for coming. I shimbled out knowing I'd been awful. I've still not heard, but at least it was good experience and I won't be as bad again.

C Footsteps in the Snow

FOOTSTEPS IN THE SNOW

Superindendant Bill Downs looked sleepily at the white covered streets of London through his office window in Scotland Yard. From his office window he had a fine view of the heart of London. He looked at the blanket of snow covering the city, lost in his own thoughts. The telephone rang and he stepped over to it, casually picking up the receiver to hear the voice of Detective Sergeant John Toyota.

"Alright John, what do you want?" he said quickly, wishing it was nothing serious.

"Well sir, I've found something very interesting. I think you should come down & see it" replied the Detective Sergeant. There was something in the tone of his voice that convinced Bill he should go.

"Alright, where are you?" Bill took the address which he recognised as an old building at the back of the Thames. He pulled on his thick over coat and took his hat from the hat stand near door, switching the light off before rushing down the stairs to his car just outside the building.

He arrived at the building in about ten minutes, and realized something important had happened, because of the ambulance and the group of reporters awaiting his arrival. As soon as he opened the door of his car he was greeted with a barrage of questions.

"Sorry, don't know what has happened myself yet" he said, as he dismissed them in his ~~usually~~ usual polite manner. He didn't particularly like the press, but he knew they were only doing their job and he also realised that it was a good idea to keep on good ~~relationship~~ relations with them.

He walked over to the stretcher ^on the ground^ and pulled the blanket back from over the face, it was ~~an old~~ a young mans face slightly distorted but Bill recognised him as Cliff Mason, a ~~young~~ young sergeant who had shown great promise in his successful but short ~~career~~ career.

"He was killed by three stab wounds, all in the heart", it was John Temple who had come over as soon as seeing Bill arrive. "But what I called you out for is over here" ~~John~~ continued John. He pointed to the bank of the Thames and ushered Bill over nearly slipping in his excitement.

Bill Down's face set grimly, he saw in front of him a thing he had secretly ~~feared~~ feared ^almost^ for exactly a year. He looked down and ^saw^ a set of footprints marked clearly in the snow, but what was unusual was that one footprint was about a size 11 ~~men~~ and the other the size of an infants shoe. Bill thought back to last winter five policemen killed on duty in one month. There had been a public ~~outcry~~, but one policeman had caught ~~the~~ the murderer in the act. He had chased him in the car and the murderer had skidded on the ice and gone over the side of the hill, his car bursting in flames, but there had been no trace of a body and Bill Downs had secretly feared the cop killer to be alive, now his fears had become realisation.

Bill picked up the file of Cliff Mason and read through it, what a waste he thought, Cliff Mason had had a perfect record and was already soon on line for another promotion, Bill studied the file, nothing, he was looking for anything that would give him any clue, to what, he did not know, but he had picked up a sixth sense during his twenty years of police service and this sense told him everything was not what it seemed.

Bill decided to go back to the scene of the crime and look around. When he arrived he walked over to where the footprints had been the snow had melted with a surprise turn in the weather and Bill spotted something shining due to the new bright sun. It was a belt buckle, Bills heart dropped, it was nothing however he put the buckle in his pocket.

He went to his car and on his way back he stopped at a cafe for a drink of tea to warm him up. As he entered the cafe the man at the counters face looked nervous Bill recognised him as Charlie Wright an ex-copper turned bad in the force and caught pushing drugs obtained from the police department. Bill greeted the man suspiciously and ordered a cup of tea the man served it and Bill quickly drank it and left.

However something was nagging at his brain and as he felt in his pockets for his cigarrettes it clicked.

He took the belt buckle out and realised that Charlie Wright had, had a damaged buckle. Bill drove back to his office and got the file on Wright, as he had suspected the case had been solved by Sergeant Cliff Mason. Everything clicked Charlie Wright had used the disguise of the cop killer to throw them off the scent, and gain his revenge.

Bill returned to the cafe and waited outside in the car, as he suspected the now worried Charlie Wright shut his shop early and came out of the shop carrying a large brown bag. Bill ran from the car and had snatched the bag from Charlie before he knew he was there. Inside there were two shoes a large boot and a boot whose sole sloped inwards leaving the mark of a small shoe. Bill took Charlie down to the yard and booked him.

Later that night Bill looked out over the again snow covered london and relieved and with a grin of satisfaction on his face. This time no phone calls disturbed him.

D Footsteps in the Snow

Footsteps in the Snow

The driving sleet slashed the windscreen, each individual droplet causing a whiplike sound to reverberate through the cabin. Inside ① Alan Morrison gripped his steering wheel even tighter and cursed the day he took on this trans-America job. He peered forward, straining to see the road in front. The windshield was covered with a fine coating of snow, and as soon as the wipers cleared this curtain that shut out the day, it reappeared in greater strength.

As the windscreen cleared for a split-second Alan glimpsed a black void in front of the truck. As the vehicle dropped forward, his mind, working incredibly clearly, realised that the road had bent sharply to the left. He was just thinking over the implications of this fact when the world exploded around him and he passed out.

He awoke, to see the world do a somersault before slowly leveling out. He shook his head to clear it, then quickly stopped, as it nearly fell off. Slowly he pulled himself to his feet, and stood unsteadily for a while surveying his surroundings. About 20 feet away lay the remains of his truck now buried in a deep snow-drift at the foot of a small cliff. Small, but unclimbable. There was no way back to the road that way. He must have been thrown from the cabin onto the drift at the base of the tree that was towering behind him. A stray branch accounted for the ache in the small of his back.

Something was wrong. For a moment he knew that all was not quite correct, but the

reason eluded him. Footprints! All about the cab of
the truck there were footsteps. They were partly
obscured by some fall of snow but there was
no doubt that they were there and they were
human prints, not animal.

Alan hurried over to the cab and gingerly
reached inside for his lunchbox. It wasn't there.
He needed food to be able to follow the footsteps.
He would starve if he had no food. ~~Desper~~ Desperately he dug in the snow. Two or 3 inches
down he found an empty box "Damn scavengers"
he called to the sky.

The snow started to fall and Alan
realised there was no way he was going to be
able to see the footsteps if the snow continued
descending at this rate. The light would soon be
fading and then he would be stuck out in the
wild to starve to death. He began to run but
made no more progress than before. He began to
despair of any hope.

He came stumbling to a clearing. Right
in the middle the footsteps stopped abruptly.
No indentations, not the slightest indication
where he should go next. Alan Morrison, truck
driver, sat down on the snow and wept. He
did not hear the faint rustle behind him,
or the sound of feet crunching snow.

The animal snarl rang around the forest
and Alan turned swiftly. He was just in
time to see a slavering, dirty half animal-
half man swing the rusty axe. Again in this
moment of what he believed was the end, his
mind worked clearly 'This man must have been
stranded like myself,' he thought. 'Perhaps I

would have become like him. I suppose it's a question of survival, really. Dog eat dog.' In the split second he took to run over all this in his mind he watched the axe arch through the air and felt it bite into his shoulder. The vibrations ran through his body and he fell backwards. The crack of his shoulder-bone snapping still echoed inside his head. Again the axe fell, and again.

The creature stood panting over the still form in front of it. Blood seeped from wounds over its the body and stained the snow it lay on. The man-beast knelt by the corpse and picked it up with ease born of long practice. Blood ran over its hand. Putting its fingers in its mouth, the monster sucked off the blood. It turned and, picking up the axe, lumbered off into the ever deepening snow.

ESSAYS

E A Working Day in the Life of a School Caretaker

<u>A working day in the life of a school caretaker</u>

Fred scrambled out of bed, weary eyed and depressed with the thought of the day ahead. His wife rose and shuffled into the kitchen to make Freds breakfast. She seemed still asleep and looked as though she was spreading the butter, pouring the tea and slicing the toast unconsciously as if from memory.

Fred ate his breakfast and skipped through the paper, neither he or his wife speaking to each other. He looked closely at an article, in his paper, on the <u>bannishment</u> of the strap "Nothing new" he mumbled to himself "they've been saying that it will be banned since I began my job."

He looked at his watch, half past eight, and decided that against his better judgement he best go and inspect the school before the rabble arrive. He unconsciously kissed his wife goodbye and strode out of the door.

The cold, wintery air hit his face and he paused to watch the cars speed past, and the horns blowing and the abuse thrown at each other. Then he thought to himself "Not such a bad job after all." Thinking on this matter he pulled a cigarette out of his creased packet and he skilfully lit it against the blowing wind, a thing learnt after years of smoking.

He looked up and saw the first pupils arriving, he had noticed that in the first two years the pupils arrived very early but as they got older they were more often late than early.

He opened the doors and made himself ready for the sudden flow of people pouring through the door pushing, laughing, cursing none taking notice of his pleas for them to let him open the doors. After the main body of children had shoved their way in he managed to fully open

142

the doors and began to curse because it had begun to rain which meant twice as much work as usual because of the dirt they would tread in with them.

Monday morning always began with assembly, so, Fred thought, he would be able to check the boilers and repair the broken desks Mrs Brown had told him about in room 105. The boilers were okay and the desks just needed a few new screws to secure them.

It was now ten o'clock and it was time for him to go back to his house, next to the school, and have a 'cupper' before the tanker with the oil arrived. He was just leaving when a shrill voice "Er, excuse me Fred'ick", he hated that name, and only one teacher ever called it him, Mrs George from home economics. "Can you clean the blackboard in my room," she went on "it's ever so dirty".

He went to his shed and got his spray for cleaning blackboards and after he had done this, Mrs Jones, the music teacher, caught him with the spray and asked him to do her room as well. This he did, then he rushed down and met the tanker arriving at the school gates. The unloading of the tanker was a lengthy process and, a dirty one. By the time it had been unloaded, and he had cleaned himself, it was afternoon break.

He walked through the playground not noticed by many, except the smokers who came rushing over asking for a cigarette with promises of, "I'll give you two back tomorrow." He dismissed them, to their curses, with a shake of the head.

All that needed doing now was to repair the five-a-side nets in the sportshall, which he did promptly and expertly.

The joyful ring of the bell hit his ears and he

watched the children rushing out of school and clambering onto the busses buses. He welcomed the cleaning ladies with a toothless grin and went round the school checking for damage. Luckily there was none and he retired home for his tea at half past six and was greeted by his wife. This time there was no lack of conversation.

F Circuses and Zoos should be Forbidden – They are Cruel to Animals

Circuses and zoos should be forbidden. They are cruel to animals.

Circuses and zoos have been very popular, and still are. They provide excellent entertainment for people of many ages. However, for many years naturalists have argued that circuses and zoos are cruel and that it is not natural for an animal to spend its lifetime in captivity. These people believe it to be much better for the animal if it was to be left in the wild and allowed to fend for itself, as it was undoubtedly meant to.

However, there are also numerous arguments against this. One of these is that for many kinds of animals it is necessary. One such animal is the Giant Panda. This animal only breeds in China and therefore there cannot be many of them. If they were allowed to breed purely in China then all it would take for these animals to become rapidly extinct would be a famine, perhaps a very harsh summer, whereas if there were more animals in different parts of the world obviously all of them would not be affected so leaving more of the animals alive. This can only benefit the animals.

In the case of some animals, like chimpanzees, and numerous other types of monkey, they enjoy performing in the circus ring and making people laugh and enjoy themselves. This kind of animal are able to build up relationships with their owner or trainer akin to that built up by man and his dog. A dog enjoys living with humans and working with humans and nobody, I am sure, would say anything to the contrary. Therefore, if a dog can enjoy this relationship why should any other animal be different. If the animals enjoy circus life then surely these institutions cannot be cruel and should not be forbidden.

Very few zoos can be said to be cruel places. Compared to the life the animals would lead in the wild the animals in the zoo lead a life of great luxury. They are fed regularly and have possibly better meals than they could ever have had if they were forced to hunt for their own food in the wild. They encounter (danger) no danger at all and are never under threat of death from another animal. Therefore, surely they must lead a much longer, happier life than if they were free to roam the wild.

The other side to the argument has been argued by naturalists for

145

many years, however. Their argument is basically that it is cruel for animals to live in a zoo or circus which are so unlike their natural habitat. They say that it is cruel to keep them cooped up in a cage when they want to follow their natural instincts which are to roam and be given a free hand in deciding what to do. In a zoo they are fed and everything is done for them. All they do is sit around the cage and mooch. Even if they are fed regularly and are safe from any wild predators, to do nothing in a cage all their life except sit down or perhaps walk around the perimeter, which cannot be far, is not very healthy. An animal that, under normal circumstances, would have to kill for its food would mean it has an awful lot of exercise. It just isn't possible or practical to give animals from a zoo the kind of exercise that is necessary to keep them in peak physical condition. (An unfit anim) I don't think you could imagine a zoo keeper taking a couple of rhinoceros, elephants and tigers for a run round the park like you can with a dog. I think this would cause rather a stir in the neighbourhood. Therefore, no matter how well the animals are looked after by the zoo keeper, the animals must obviously be unfit which can only lead to a shortened life. This completely cancels out the argument that zoos are necessary for animals that are on the verge of extinction.

¶ Circuses are possibly even more detrimental to an animal's nature than a zoo. There is only one possible method of teaching a wild animal to do tricks and that method is cruelty. It is the only thing that a wild animal can understand. It wouldn't be practical to attempt to lure a tiger to do a trick by enticing it with (a) some meat as it would probably take the meat and you aswell. You couldn't stroke it and pet it as it would also probably turn upon you. One method of cruelty that is in great evidence in circuses is the great use of the whip. It is very rare that you see an animal trainer in a circus go into the ring without his whip. The animal recognises it as a means of inflicting pain and therefore cowers away from it. Once the animal is afraid the trainer realises it is under his power and can then proceed to make it do his bidding. Hence the unnatural sight of a tiger jumping through a flaming hoop.

The only possible solution to this dilemna would be to transport the animals to the different countries, but instead of putting them in circuses and zoos to put them in reservations and allow them to live like they do in their natural home. An example of such an institution is Knowsley Safari Park, but even here the animals do not roam freely, although they do have more (~~too much~~) freedom than in a zoo or circus, as they are not allowed to mix with other animals and are still fed with the help of humans.

However, this is a much kinder way than leaving the animals cooped up in circuses and zoos to die unhappily.

Approaches to different types of essays

Most Examining Bodies give a reasonably wide choice of topics. The Examiners' aim is to provide subjects that will produce a variety of writing styles. If you look at a typical examination paper you will find that the list of essays includes a topic that is mainly descriptive, one that is narrative, one that asks for an opinion, and possibly one that is imaginative or capable of being dealt with in any of the three ways. The following are hints on how to approach the different types of essays, but, *note*, these categories are not self-contained; there is much overlapping. A narrative may contain description, but if you are asked for a straightforward description you should not turn it into a narrative. Most personal essays are a mixture of the categories: e.g.

What are your own views on corporal punishment in schools? *or*
How I spend Saturdays

Descriptive

A good description relies upon careful observation and is something you can train yourself in. What you write should be clear and vivid whether the subject matter is realistic (i.e. attempting to describe the object or person as it really is) or imaginative. Good descriptions tend to be a mixture of the overall view with detail added.

Scenes or places

You should first decide on the overall impression that you wish to create and then make detailed notes on as many relevant observations as you can, such as the colour, action, movement and atmosphere of the scene. Then select, order and develop those details in the best way to achieve the effect that you have in mind. The tone of the words you choose should be consistent with the mood or atmosphere that you are seeking. Vary the focus of your description; that is, as with good camera work, you should vary background shots with close-ups, as well as featuring action in the middle ground.

Exercises

Write paragraphs, 15 to 20 lines long, on the following:

1 The contrast between the pictures opposite.

2 Snow in the town

3 A mountain scene

4 Motorway scenery viewed from a car at speed

5 A deserted and wind-swept shopping precinct

6 A park at night

7 Houses awaiting demolition

8 A well-kept or overgrown garden

People

This involves similar powers of observation and even more care in shaping the portrait or character sketch that you wish to present. Physical features, clothing, posture, mannerisms or habits, movements, speech, past history, activities and occupation, incidents, and the reactions of other people to the person concerned, can prompt a wealth of ideas. However, a list such as above can produce a boring 'identikit' unless the really telling impressions are selected, and insignificant details omitted. Successful descriptions of people are often almost caricatures, that is, they emphasise certain features at the expense of others.

Exercises

Write descriptions of the following.
Organise your material into stages for para-graphing, e.g. impressions; the character revealed more closely; an illustrative incident involving the person; how others behave towards the person; he/she pictured in action at work; a meeting with the individual concerned. The order of these can obviously be rearranged, but you should aim for a progressive revelation of the character.

1 Someone you used to dislike who is now a friend

2 A local eccentric

3 A favourite relative

4 People in the bus queue

5 First boyfriend/girlfriend

6 A famous pop star

7 A famous sports star

8 Two teachers, one from primary school and the other from secondary school

Crowd scenes and events

Although these could be narrative, they are sometimes accompanied by instructions to write a description and not a story. In such writings a descrip-tion of the setting, and the place, and the people concerned needs careful balancing and blending in order to avoid disorder in handling a possibly rambling subject. Paragraph your writing into clear stages of development, e.g. opening scene; action sequence; a climax to the event; and the place after the event.
Sometimes the title limits you to only part of this sequence. Write about one of the following:

Exercises

1 Pop concert or festival

2 Rush hour

3 Miss World or Mr Universe contest

4 A public meeting or political demonstration

5 Morning assembly

6 An amusement arcade at night

7 The local take-away or chip shop

8 An outdoor market on a winter's day

9 One of the pictures on page 151.

Vocabulary

1 Adjectives are obviously of great importance in writing descriptions. Try to vary the words which are merely physical, e.g. dark, swarthy, with words that create mood or attitude, e.g. sombre. Hyphenated adjectives can be very useful but should not be overdone, e.g. greeny-grey sea.

2 Actions and mannerisms call for a different type of word and you should consult a thesaurus in order to help you with choice of adjectives, verbs or adverbs.

151

Narrative

A narrative either tells a story or gives an account of a sequence of actions.

1 Stories need events, people, a scene, and possibly dialogue.

2 The order of events is most important. The easiest to handle is obviously the order in which they happen so that the beginning, middle and end occur chronologically. However, there can be variations of this.

The beginning

This is often the most difficult for any type of essay as it is too easy to sit looking at a blank page and wasting time. Here are some possible ways of starting a narrative essay:

1 straight into action, e.g.
   'With an unbelievable bang the lorry crashed through the front room.'

2 by an arresting, or unusual, detail, e.g.
   'It was a bright cold day in April and the clocks were striking 13.'

3 by setting the scene of the story. The danger to avoid here is that of making it too long so that you have not sufficient time to develop it.

4 by dialogue, e.g.
   'If I ever see you again,' he hissed, *'I will kill you.'*

The middle or substance of the narrative

Try to introduce a variety of events and make them a development of the introduction.

The ending

There should be a satisfying sense of ending to the story, particularly if it is about a problem. Some modern writers like to leave the story ending in mid-air, but this is very difficult to achieve satisfactorily. Do not try it until you have mastered the art of rounding off a story.

Characters

Develop the characters by:
1 their actions
2 description of their appearance
3 description of their personality
4 speech and thoughts

Dialogue

1 Vary the verbs of saying and adverbs that go with the verbs. Again a thesaurus will help you.
2 The punctuation of dialogue can be very tricky. Pay particular attention to it.
3 Remember to start on a new line for each new speaker.

Narrative assignments

1 Use the following as starting-points for narratives of your own.

   a) The fog was thick and still, muffling the cars that rolled past us with their yellow headlamps. Although we had walked home this way many times, gradually I realised that it was some time since we had blundered past an object that was familiar to us . . .

   b) 'One day it'll be my turn,' said Julia, quietly.

2 Attempt a humorous narrative which parodies elements of traditional vampire tales and builds from the following opening: (Research and plan your material carefully.)

   . . . My suspicion was first aroused by the discovery of a rather sharp set of dentures, languishing in an all-too-pink tumblerful of Steradent . . .

3 Write narratives which include these ingredients:

   a) a ferocious dog, a door-to-door salesman, a strong wind, and an unexpected ending.

   b) an eerie opening, two very different characters, an explosive incident, and an amusing conclusion.

4 Write a short story which ends with one of the following:

   a) 'For the sake of experience it was worth it, but I wouldn't want to face it again.'

   b) 'And so it ended as it had all begun: two silent figures, a flickering fire, and a record playing quietly in the background.'

   c) 'If only I had remembered.'

   d) 'He raced down the street, delight written on his face . . . Free at last.'

   e) 'The following day her lodgings were found deserted. Any incriminating evidence had vanished with her.'

5 Write a story to illustrate one of the following:
   a) A sheep in wolves' clothing
   b) A bird in the hand is worth two in the bush
   c) Too many cooks spoil the broth

6 Produce a 'science fiction' story entitled:
   a) Stranded in Galaxy 9, *or*
   b) Ten Minutes to Zero Hour, *or*
   c) What happened when the repair-itself machine broke down

7 Write a chapter from the memoirs of one of the following:
   a) a dentist
   b) a fortune teller
   c) a beautician

8 With comedy in mind, narrate an episode from history, 'correcting the records' from firsthand experience. e.g.
   'What really happened to the Spanish Armada'
   'History's debt to Eric Smith: little known pioneer of aviation'
   'The day the wheel was invented'

9 Write on one of the titles below:
   a) A mystery epidemic
   b) The warning that came too late
   c) A day trip to remember

10 Write a story suggested to you by the picture on the page opposite.

11 Writing in the first person, relate the experiences of someone running in a local marathon race for the first time. Make use of the picture sequence on page 153.

Presenting an opinion

The following extract is one student's opinion on the subject of smoking as an issue of national concern.

'Despite all the medical evidence which shows that the habit of smoking is totally unhealthy, contributing to heart disease, lung cancer and chronic bronchitis, we still do not have a government prepared to take firm action to really tackle the problem.

5   It simply is not enough to enforce health warnings on cigarette packets, to restrict smoking on public transport and in cinemas, and to ban cigarette advertisements from television. Similarly, the feeble half a million pounds that the government spent in a campaign against smoking in 1979 had little impact compared to the *fifty* millions spent by tobacco firms in the same year

10   on other forms of advertising: for example, sponsoring all manner of sporting events from snooker to Grand Prix motor racing.

The government's problem, of course, is that much as they might like to prevent smoking, they badly need the massive sums of money that they gain from high taxes on cigarettes. If only the present government had the nerve

15   to spend the large amounts needed to persuade people not to smoke (especially the young). In the long term we might *save* money that business firms and the National Health Service *lose* at present because of working days lost and the cost of treating illnesses due to smoking.

Personally, I would favour a total ban on this foul anti-social habit. Give

20   the tobacco firms a deadline of ten years to invest their great profits else- where, and rescue the weak-willed cigarette addicts from ill-health by making smoking illegal!'

Whether or not you agree with the views expressed, note several features of the author's approach:

1 **paragraphing which attempts an orderly development of ideas:**

INTRODUCTION   Para. 1 – the issue presented

BALANCED   Para. 2 – what are seen as inadequate attempts
DEVELOPMENT   made to tackle the problem

Para. 3 – why this is so, and how progress might
be made

CONCLUSION   Para. 4 – final recommendations

2 **a tidy summarising of relevant information**, most important in a short assignment, that gives authority to the opinion that follows: e.g. various government actions to curb smoking are condensed into one opening sen- tence in the second paragraph – before being criticised.

3 **persuasive tactics which seek to shape the reader's response:**
   a) the use of **emotive vocabulary** (consider the choice of: totally (line 2); chronic (line 2); feeble (line 7); foul (line 19); weak-willed (line 21); . . . and even 'of course' (line 12)).
   b) **statistics selected to impress** (e.g. the extreme contrast made between advertising expenditure to promote tobacco and the lesser sum spent by government in campaigning against smoking).

4 **language which signposts the author's intentions:**
   a) the topic sentence which opens the final paragraph;
   b) 'Similarly' (line 7) . . . indicating further evidence to support the previous statement;
   c) 'Despite' (line 1) . . . introducing a contrast.

Exercises

Treating your own choice of subject with similar care, write about a page and a half on one of the following.

1 In your local newspaper there has been some correspondence on the usefulness of space programmes. Below is the final paragraph from one of the letters.

'In short, space exploration by both Americans and Russians has achieved very little. Monstrous amounts of money have been wasted on dangerous missions for the sake of national pride, a few blurred photographs, and some dubious rock specimens. The money would have been better spent on relieving Third World poverty.'

Give your own opinion on the subject, commenting on the above extract if you wish.

2 'The death penalty should be reintroduced to protect the public and the police from terrorists and other armed criminals.'

Discuss this statement, showing how far you agree or disagree.

3 Write a contribution for or against the following motion for debate:

'Pop concerts are a nuisance: the so-called music is loud and tuneless; the use of illegal drugs is encouraged; crowds of over-excited and ill-behaved fans, dressed in outrageous clothes, are a danger to themselves and to the safety of others.'

4 'TELEVISION'S INSTANT ENTERTAINMENT IS TO BLAME FOR KIDS WHO HAVE NO LEISURE INTERESTS'

'EXPERIMENTS ON ANIMALS VITAL FOR PROGRESS PROCLAIMS TOP SCIENTIST'

Choose one of these newspaper headlines and say how far you agree with the statement made.

Using diagrams to develop an essay

The following diagrams show you one way of developing an essay or talk on a given subject. First you write down a word covering the whole area and then at random write down as many words or phrases which indicate ideas related to the original word. Make this radiate outwards as in the diagram, then take each of these new words and see if it is capable of being extended. You will eventually have a lot of information; some of it will be relevant, some of it will not. You have to select what you need and arrange the information into a logical order.

Exercises

1 Study the diagrams and say how some of the end words can be developed.

Diagram A

2 If you had a talk or essay on the topic 'Should sport be a compulsory subject in schools?', which of the information could you use?

3 Use the diagram to write an essay or give a talk on the topic 'Sport is a means of establishing friendships between countries'.

Diagram B

4 Which of the material would you use in a talk or essay on 'Fashion is an important part of the economy'?

5 Write an essay on the topic 'Fashion in clothes controls our lives more than we like to admit'.

Diagram C

6 Give a descriptive account of 'A Street Fire'.

General

7 Construct diagrams using the following as centre words:
War; Applying for a Job; My Friends; Nuclear Disarmament; Pop Music; Electronic Games; Horoscopes

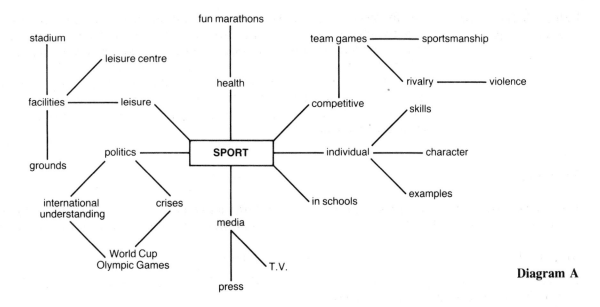

Diagram A

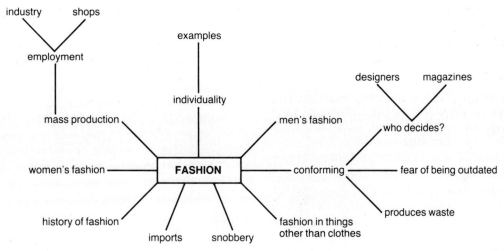

Diagram B

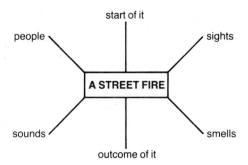

Diagram C

Structured essays

It is common practice now for Examining Boards to give help to the candidate by providing him with a number of details on a topic. This helps to overcome the freezing of mind which examination conditions create in some candidates.

Note the following:

1 The information given will probably not be in a logical order. Sort it out into connected groups.

2 You do not have to use the information given; you can use it merely as a starting point.

3 You do not have to agree with the information given. If you disagree with it use your disagreement to develop your own ideas.

Exercises

1 Read these varied opinions on aspects of **under-age drinking**, then write an essay on the subject structured as follows:

a) the nature of the problem;

b) who, or what, is responsible for the problem;

c) how, if possible, matters might be improved.

TEENAGER   You cannot blame us for drinking in pubs. There are very few places to meet: no coffee bars that open late, only youth clubs that offer little interest.

PARENTS   Today's under-age drinkers are the alcoholics of tomorrow. There is no real control over the sale of drink. Supermarkets will serve anybody. Advertisers don't help by making the drinking of alcohol so attractive.

TEACHER   Parents are largely to blame. Most teenagers are allowed to attend parties where alcohol is available, and most parents aren't bothered if their children spend money on drink.

PUBLICAN   Publicans and off-licence owners cannot really be expected to know who is under-age or not. Girls especially often look a lot older than they are.

NEWSPAPER EDITOR   The police should be more prepared to raid public houses and to withdraw the licence of anyone who persistently serves drink to those under eighteen. If this were done there would be far less under-age drinking and vandalism.

2 The following comments have been made about **work**:

Work can be fun, and men can enjoy it; then it's not labour.

I like work; it fascinates me. I can sit and look at it for hours.

All work and no play makes Jack a dull boy.

If all the year were playing holidays, to sport would be as tedious as to work.

Work expands so as to fill the time available for its completion.

Work is the unpleasant interval between periods of leisure.

Sometimes there is a pleasure to be derived from hard work, a sense of satisfaction at having tackled and overcome a difficult task.

I don't like to have to think too much at work. If the pay is good, I'll put with boredom.

Anything worthwhile usually needs to be worked for.

Most jobs nowadays are tedious and repetitive. I should like a job where I can use my initiative and imagination.

Considering some or all or none of the comments above, write on *one* of the following:
a) The ideal job.
b) Describe 2 occasions when you worked so hard, mentally or physically, that you were exhausted. Try to make clear whether or not you enjoyed the work in each case.
c) What sort of job do you imagine you will be doing in, say, ten years' time? Describe the job and your attitude to it.
d) Describe a day in the life of an unemployed person.

3 The comments printed below are concerned with **examinations** or **assessment.** Study them and then discuss *some* of the points raised, adding points of your own in order to develop your arguments.

FATHER 'Julia stays in her room and emerges from time to time white-faced. She's under enormous pressure to get the right exam grades. Her job depends upon it.'

MOTHER 'I've promised Steven a fiver for every "O" level he passes, but he spends all his time listening to pop. He says exams do not matter. His friend left at Easter and is already earning £50 a week. It wouldn't matter so much if Steven was a girl.'

PATIENT 'I hope you've passed your exams, doctor!'

HEADMASTER 'Under continuous assessment there is knowledge not only of achievement but also of progress towards it. The syllabus and any final test necessary can be set by the teacher and so the motivation of the pupil is increased and tension and anxiety reduced. Pupils should always be assessed only on what they've been taught.'

HEADMISTRESS 'One of the greatest dangers of allowing schools to set their own examinations is that teachers may be tempted to pass a child merely because he worked hard or to help him get a job. External examinations are completely impartial and are the best bulwark against poor standards.'

LECTURER 'All that is needed is a school record, which states precisely what ground the pupil has covered, what projects he has done and exactly where he has succeeded and failed. Exams should be abolished altogether and the teachers allowed to develop school work that would genuinely engage the interest of all their pupils.'

Writing based on photographs or drawings

The following photographs, or cartoons, present a scene. Study each one closely then write an essay, or piece of continous writing, based on it. You may write a description or narrative, provided it relates to the main items of the photograph, e.g. if the photograph or picture has a historical setting then that should be part of your writing. If you were to use the photograph of the man being chased by an aeroplane, and wrote an essay on the need to keep fit, or on men's clothes, then you would receive few marks.

DECISIONS! DECISIONS!
LIFE AND CHOICE

Excerpts from the average life and the choices to be made.

1 Which rattle shall I play with?

2 Which primary school should I go to?

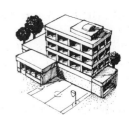

3 Which secondary school should I go to?

4 Which subjects should I choose to study?

5 Which career or job do I want to follow?

6 What options are open to me?

7 Whom shall I marry?

8 Where shall we live?

9 How many children shall we have?

10 What names shall we call them?

11 Shall we move house?

Using whatever part of the above material you find helpful, write an essay on one of the following topics:

Either
'Oh for a life without having to make decisions!'

Or
'How truly independent can we be in making decisions which affect our lives?' Base your answer on what has already happened to you and on the decisions you will have to make in the future.

163

Consider the situation in the above picture and write a description or narrative account of it.

Compose a short story or narrative in which the opposite incident plays an important part.

Use the picture opposite and that above as part of the source material for an account of EITHER Disasters in Sport OR Humour in Sport.

Facts and information

An important function of language is to give information. This function accounts for most of the language we use in everyday life and work. It is concerned with giving information, as in reports, letters, explanations, or with assessing information, as in summaries and reports. It is important, therefore, to master this use of language, not only in order to deal with the testing of it in examinations, but in order to cope with everyday life and work.

When making summaries, reports or writing in this impersonal way you must pay particular attention to:
1 the type of language used;
2 the layout.

The language used

1 Be clear and unambiguous (cf. p. 18 and 25).
2 Be accurate.
3 Be brief and to the point.
4 Make sentences as simple and straightforward as possible.
5 Be careful in choice of words (cf. p. 16 Registers, p. 18 Special vocabularies, p. 21 Words as signposts).

The layout

1 The material should be presented in an orderly, logical way.

2 Use paragraphs and sub-paragraphs.

3 In order to indicate the paragraphs and sub-paragraphs use:
   a) indenting
   b) underlining
   c) consistent numbering and lettering
   d) different spacing between topics

Now study the information leaflets on pp. 189 and 207 and assess their effectiveness using the above points as guidelines. In addition, consider the use of different type faces and the diagram.

Reports

Brochure for tourists

Write a short report, for an information brochure for tourists, on the imaginary holiday resort described in note form below. Reorganise the material provided into a fluent piece of writing (250 words approximately).

Brenton – large seaside resort on South Colston coast – wooded hills overlook extensive Brent Bay – very mild climate throughout the year – parks and gardens include subtropical vegetation – motorway and rail access – luxury hotels, caravan parks, two holiday camps, rented flats/chalets, guest houses – attractions: theatre, golf course, museum, yachting, cliff walks, two cinemas, speedway team, fishing, pony riding, underwater-swimming club, casino, art gallery, good beaches, permanent fair ground – local features: ruins of twelfth century Brenton Abbey; Stone Age relics at nearby Grantley Caves.

As a headteacher

As a headteacher, you have been asked to give information and make recommendations to a local hi-fi and record shop owner concerning four school leavers who have all applied for the recently advertised post of sales assistant at the shop.

Read closely the careers teacher's notes on the applicants and then write a confidential report to the shop owner:
1 discussing the relative merits of those who have applied for the job;
2 including your recommendation as to which one of the four would, in your view, be the most suitable for the post.

[16+ ALSEB]

Ian Stanley . . . age 18 . . . intelligent, personable, easygoing . . . occasionally unreliable. Qualifications: A levels – History, French, Music; O levels – Maths, English, French, Music, Commerce, History . . . Interests: guitarist with local group . . . Ambition: undecided . . . Work experience: nil . . . Accepted for University degree course in Music, but although full grant available parents oppose further education and would prefer Ian to be earning money . . . Family: father currently unemployed; 3 younger brothers and sisters. Ian has recently left home.

Denise Lacey . . . age 16 . . . average ability, hard-working, shy . . . smart in appearance . . . Qualifications: O levels – Maths, History, Physics; CSEs – English, Art; completed day release course in Office Skills at local technical college . . . Interests: dancing, popular music, secretary of school folk music society. . . . Ambition: to make a career as an efficient secretary . . . Work experience: part-time rack filler at local supermarket.

David Shields . . . age 16 . . . bright, practical, little interest in academic pursuits . . . Qualifications: CSEs – English, Maths, Geography . . . has been offered electrical apprenticeship . . . Interests: electronics, football, rock music . . . Work experience: serving in his father's bookshop . . . Indifferent school attendance record . . . Several reprimands for insolence to teachers in first two years at school.

Suzanne Gibson . . . age 17 . . . average ability yet good results by virtue of sheer determination . . . extrovert, stubborn . . . Qualifications: O levels – Art, English, Maths, Domestic Science, French; currently taking A level courses in Art, English Literature and Domestic Science . . . Decision to leave school mid-course very much a surprise . . . Interests: painting, travel, classical music . . . Family: would prefer Suzanne to complete her courses, yet don't feel that they can persuade her to stay . . . Suzanne has recently been made a school prefect . . . One minor conviction for shop-lifting (aged 14).

173

Alcohol and petrol

The driver of the vehicle shown in the photograph above was 19 years of age. He stole the car and drove round several towns, stopping periodically for a drink.

The car failed to negotiate a slight left-hand bend and collided with a lamp post. Prior to the collision the speed of the vehicle was estimated at 75 mph. Needless to say he died.

PC John Brown of the Rochdale traffic unit was the reporting officer.

Conclusion:

The driver had consumed far too much alcohol to be driving. Because of the manner in which the vehicle was being driven, a passenger had left the driver quite some time prior to the accident to walk the several miles to his home.

1 Suppose you were the passenger involved. Give an account to PC John Brown of what happened before you left the car.

2 Write out the official report by PC Brown giving all the information he had.

Electrical appliances

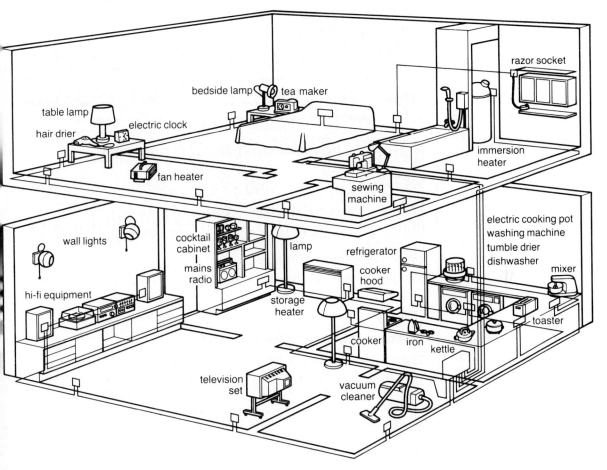

The diagram shows the range of electrical appliances that could be found in the house.

1 Suppose that you were told that there were too many and that you had to get rid of two from the upper level and four from the lower level. Write out in note form, using paragraphs, sub-paragraphs and sentences, the appliances you would discard and why.

Or

2 Write a report, or article, on the topic 'Do we depend too much on electricity in our everyday lives at home?' Use the diagram as a basis for your report.

Royal Pennine Show

A group of pupils from your school intends to visit the Royal Pennine Show and you have been asked to arrange the visit. Study the programme below and the plan.

Write a report indicating the special attractions of the show for the group concerned. Include in it suggestions about possible meeting places and a timetable for the visit so that you might cater for different interests.

ROYAL PENNINE SHOW PROGRAMME

GRAND RING EVENTS

12.00	Band of Grenadier Guards
1.00	Parade of New Agricultural Machinery
2.00	Show Jumping
3.15	Presentation of Show Jumping awards by the Queen Mother
3.45	Hevisi War Drums and Dancers from Ceylon
4.30	Fox-hound Parade
5.00	Red Devils Parachute Jump
5.30	Band of Grenadier Guards

All other Judging Events outside Grand Ring start at 3.45 and are expected to last an hour.

Entrance Charge to Ground – £1.00; Students – 50p; Grand Ring – 50p

---

16+ (ALSEB) Paper 1

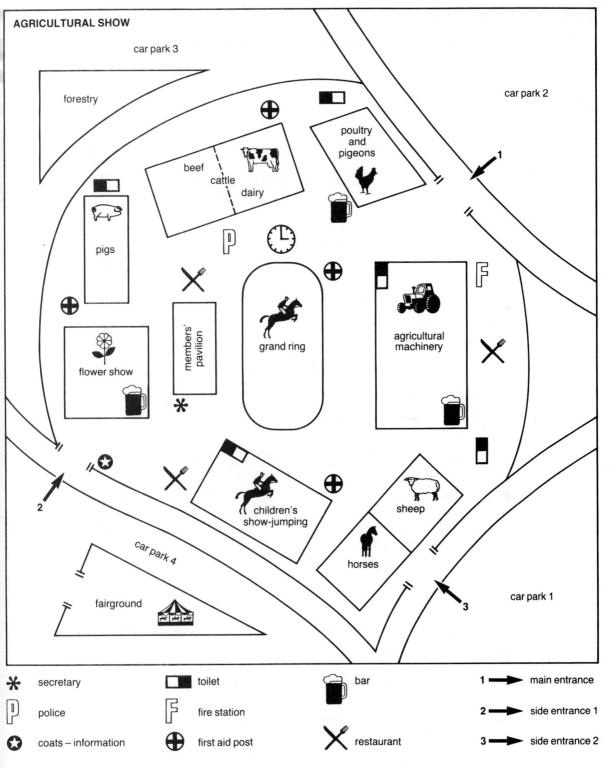

AGRICULTURAL SHOW

✳	secretary	
ℙ	police	
✪	coats – information	

▭	toilet
𝔽	fire station
⊕	first aid post

🍺	bar
✕	restaurant

1 →	main entrance
2 →	side entrance 1
3 →	side entrance 2

A day out at Heaton Park

Suppose you are responsible for arranging an outing for a group of people to Heaton Park. The group is composed of adults and children (aged 7–14). Study the plan and then draw up two suggested itineraries for:

a) the adults

b) the children

The outing should last three hours.

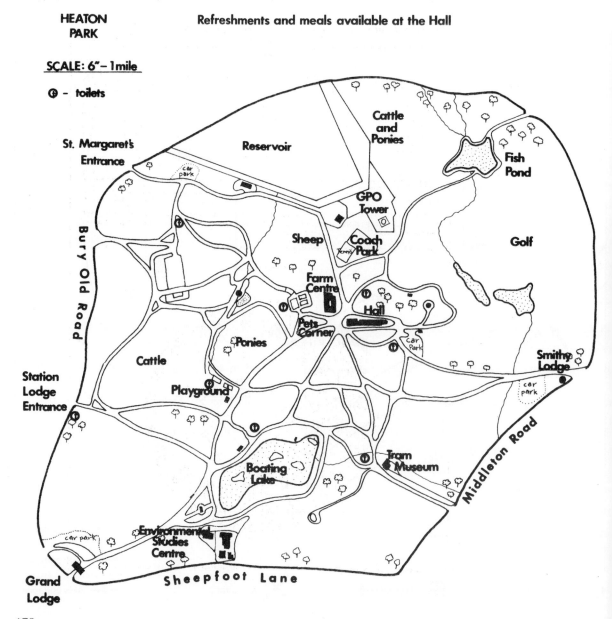

HEATON PARK

Refreshments and meals available at the Hall

SCALE: 6" – 1 mile

🚻 - toilets

St. Margaret's Entrance

Reservoir

Cattle and Ponies

Fish Pond

Bury Old Road

GPO Tower

Sheep

Coach Park

Golf

Farm Centre

Hall

Pets Corner

Ponies

Cattle

Smithy Lodge

Station Lodge Entrance

Playground

Tram Museum

Boating Lake

Middleton Road

Environmental Studies Centre

Grand Lodge

Sheepfoot Lane

Fires in the home

Study the accompanying table and diagram and then write a brief article entitled 'Fires in the Home'.

In your article discuss the following:

a) the main causes of domestic fires in different parts of the home and how such causes compare;

b) why fires are more common at certain times of day;

c) precautions that might be taken to prevent accidental fires in the home.

Table 12.11   Domestic[1] fires: by cause and room of origin, 1976[2]

United Kingdom   Percentages and thousands

Cause:	Kitchen	Bedroom[3]	Living room	Hall[4]	Roof space	Elsewhere[5] or not known	Number of fires (= 100%) (thousands)
Cooking	99	1	–	–	–	–	17·4
Space heating	9	25	42	3	–	21	5·6
Smoking materials	8	39	32	2	–	18	3·8
Children	3	30	10	5	1	50	3·3
Wiring installation	13	13	10	17	5	42	3·1
Chimneys[6]	8	16	17	1	15	42	1·7
TV and radio	1	3	91	–	–	4	1·7
Other	19	22	12	5	3	38	14·2
Total all causes	42	15	15	3	2	22	50·9

The columns labelled "Percentage started in:" span Kitchen, Bedroom[3], Living room, Hall[4], Roof space, and Elsewhere[5] or not known.

[1] Residential houses, flats and maisonettes; and living accommodation as part of another occupancy.   [2] Provisional data.   [3] Includes bed-sitting rooms.   [4] Includes stairs and corridors.   [5] Includes fires which started outside and spread to the building.   [6] Excludes fires confined to chimneys.

Source: UK Fire Statistics, Home Office

Table 12.11 is a new table showing the causes and room of origin of domestic fires to which the fire service was called. The most common room in which a fire started in 1976 was the kitchen, and cooking was the most common single cause of fires.

Chart 12.12   Domestic[1] fire calls: by hour of day, 1976[2]

United Kingdom

[1] Residential houses, flats and maisonettes, and living accommodation as part of another occupancy.   [2] Provisional data.

Souce: UK Fire Statistics, Home Office

The Sun Centre

Here is the diagram of a sun centre. Using the information given draw up leaflets designed to attract:
1 youth clubs;
2 family groups.

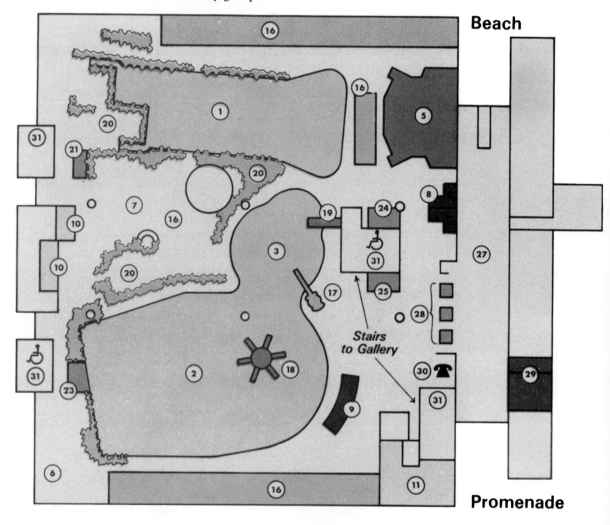

KNOW YOUR WAY AROUND!

IT'S ALL UNDER ONE ROOF
AT THE GIANT FUN'N'SUN CENTRE ON THE PROM!

① Surfing Pool

② Tropical Lagoon

③ Children's Splash Pool

④ Roof Top Monorail

⑤ Model 'GRAND PRIX'
Racing Circuit

⑥ Poolside 'SUN-TAN' Beds

⑦ Tropical Island Entertainment Area

⑧ Entrance to Changing Rooms
(1,000 individual lockers)

⑨ Entrance to Pool from
changing rooms

⑩ Licensed Island Bar and Snack Bar

⑪ Terrace Snack Bar

⑫ Bridge and Viewing
Gallery Walk-way

⑬ Gallery Lounge Bar (Licensed)

⑭ Gallery Cafeteria

⑮ Sunset Licensed Restaurant

⑯ Areas of seating

⑰ Pink Elephant

⑱ Friendly Octopus

⑲ Water Chute

⑳ Tropical Vegetation Areas

㉑ Ice Cream Kiosk

㉒ Ice Cream Kiosk (Gallery level)

㉓ T-Shirt Kiosk and Gift Shop

㉔ Confectionery Kiosk

㉕ Beachwear Kiosk

㉖ Control Centre Tower

㉗ The Mall - A 'walk-through'
from the Promenade to the Beach

㉘ Entrance Kiosks

㉙ Office of Reception
and Commissionaires

㉚ Telephones

㉛ Toilets

♿ Toilet & Changing Room facilities
available, ground floor level.

OPEN ALL DAY, EVERY DAY, EVENINGS TOO,
ALL SUMMER SEASON
APRIL - SEPTEMBER 27th
(10a.m. - 11p.m.)
Then MOST WINTER WEEKENDS
(Friday late afternoon and evenings,
Saturday and Sunday)

FOR DETAILS OF
FREE EVENING ENTERTAINMENT
AND FAMILY COMPETITIONS
ON THE TROPICAL ISLAND –
SEE PROGRAMME AT ENTRANCE

School subjects

A few years ago several thousand parents were asked the question: 'Which school subjects are very important for your child to learn at school?'

In the tables printed below the subjects (or groups of subjects) are listed on the left and the percentages of parents who thought they were very important are recorded opposite them on the right. The first table records the opinions of boys' parents. The second table records the opinions of girls' parents.

Study the tables carefully. Think about the value you and your friends place on different school subjects. Compare this with that of parents recorded here. Then write an article for a school magazine on the topic:

Are children and their parents agreed about what should be taught in schools today?

16+ (ALSEB)

PARENTS
Proportions considering that various school subjects were very important for their child to learn at school.

Boys

%

Subject	%
English (including reading, writing, spelling)	91
Mathematics (including arithmetic)	91
Metalwork, woodwork, technical drawing and other technical subjects like these	71
Physical education, things like athletics gymnastics, games and swimming	68
Geography	54
Current affairs, social studies	45
Religious instruction	43
Science subjects like chemistry, physics, biology, rural science and general science	40
History	28
Foreign languages	28
Music, arts and crafts, and subjects like basketwork, drawing, painting, pottery and weaving	24
Cookery, housecraft, mothercraft, needlework and domestic subjects like these	17
Typing, shorthand, bookkeeping and commercial subjects like these	13

Girls

%

Subject	%
Cookery, housecraft, mothercraft, needlework and domestic subjects like these	92
English (including reading, writing, spelling)	90
Mathematics (including arithmetic)	86
Physical education, things like athletics gymnastics, games and swimming	59
Typing, shorthand, bookkeeping and commercial subjects like these	54
Geography	47
Religious instruction	45
Current affairs, social studies	41
Foreign languages	31
History	29
Music, arts and crafts, and subjects like basketwork, drawing, painting, pottery and weaving	28
Science subjects like chemistry, physics, biology, rural science and general science	24
Metalwork, woodwork, technical drawing and other technical subjects like these	7

183

Extracting information and summaries

There is a variety of different types of précis you may be asked to do. Sometimes you are given a passage and asked to reduce it to a prescribed length. On other occasions you are asked merely to extract various items of information from the passage. This new type of precis or summarising is much more relevant to your future needs in employment.

Outline or skeleton

1 Read the passage through without stopping. It often helps to summarise in one sentence what the passage is about.

2 If the passage is divided into paragraphs number each paragraph consecutively and write down against the number what the general topic of the paragraph is. Often there will be a key sentence which will indicate this.

3 If the passage is not divided into paragraphs then make your own divisions and then carry on as for No. 2.

4 Now consider each paragraph individually and extract from it the supporting arguments or ideas. Indicate what they are by short words or phrases. Number them accordingly: e.g.
   a) variety of fashions in modern dress
      i) teenagers
      ii) older people
   b) influence of shops on fashion
      i) small boutiques
      ii) multiple stores

5 If the writer gives a list of supporting examples try to bring them together in a word or phrase which adequately embraces them all, e.g. a list of items such as knives, forks, spoons, corkscrews, pots, pans, food mixers, could be summarised as household utensils.

6 You should now have an adequate outline or skeleton of the passage in note form. The next step is to write it out in full, connected sentences. Do not forget the importance of words which indicate the direction of the way a discussion or description is going (cf., pp. 21). If a number of words is stipulated then make sure you do not exceed it. If the examination instructions state: 'Summarise the following passage in not more than 100 words' and you use more than 100, the extra words will be ignored.

Key sentences

A key or topic sentence in a paragraph is one that comes closest to pin-pointing the purpose or subject of the paragraph as a whole. In well-ordered writing, these often occur as a paragraph's opening or concluding sentence. In the paragraphs below, they are not so obviously placed. Find and discuss what you consider to be the key sentence in each paragraph.

1 Travelling to work that morning proved difficult. In fact it proved to be the final straw. On arriving at the station, I discovered that a rail strike meant that my train was cancelled. I trudged to the bus stop, only to hover miserably for twenty minutes while being drenched by a shower of sleet, before the bus turned up. When I eventually reached the office, I was lectured for poor timekeeping by a supervisor. Shivering with cold and furious at the injustice, I flung a sodden briefcase at him. Needless to say, I was asked to resign.

2 On an afternoon in September a woman came into the jeweller's shop. The two assistants, whose bodies had contrived, as human bodies doggedly will, to adapt the straight, hard stretch of the glass showcases to a support, sagged, hips thrust forward, elbows leaning in upon their black *crêpe-de-Chine*-covered stomachs, and looked at her without a flicker, waiting for her to go. For they could see that she did not belong there. No woman in a frayed and shapeless old Leg-horn hat, carrying a bulging crash shopping-bag, decorated in church bazaar fashion with wool embroidery, and wearing stained old sandshoes and cheap thick pink stockings that concertinaed round her ankles, could belong in the jeweller's shop. They knew the kind; simple, a bit dazed, short-sighted, and had wandered in mistaking it for the chemist's two doors up. She would peer round stupidly, looking as if she had stumbled into Aladdin's cave, and when she saw the handsome canteens of cutlery, with their beautifully arranged knives spread like a flashing keyboard in their velvet beds, and the pretty little faces of the watches in their satin cases, and the cool, watering preening of the cut glass beneath its special light, she would mumble and shamble herself out again. So they stood, unmoved, waiting for her to go.

A Present for a Good Girl Nadine Gordimer

3 The Earth's stocks of traditional fuels are rapidly being exhausted. Coal, gas and oil will in time disappear. Fuel prices are outstripping the general rate of inflation, much to the annoyance of the domestic consumer. Thus the attractions of forms of energy which appear to be free become increasingly appealing. Some enterprising home-owners are investing in equipment to harness solar energy. Others are turning to wind power, developing new forms of the traditional windmill – where local conditions are suitable.

Paragraphing and development

Consider the three-paragraph passage that follows, concerning the activities of flies; then discuss the questions on the passage's ideas and their development.

The main danger from flies is the spread of disease. The feet of flies are equipped with special sticky cushions which pick up bits of almost anything that they land on. This can contaminate food with unpleasant bacteria and even the eggs of parasite worms.

5 The fly also spreads disease by its method of eating. Gastric juices are regurgitated from the stomach on to solid food to liquefy it. The fly then sucks up this liquid mush into its stomach. In this way the various foods that the fly visits can become cross-contaminated.

In the past the house fly played a part in spreading typhoid, dysentery,
10 and probably polio. But with major changes in sanitation that have taken place flies no longer have the same opportunity to transmit such serious diseases. However their habits still allow them to pass on to humans various gastro-enteric illnesses.

1 Which sentence in the extract contains the most effective statement of the subject of the passage as a whole?

2 Why does the author begin a new paragraph? (line 5)

3 Why might paragraph 2 be regarded as a more logical successor to paragraph 1, than paragraph 3 is to paragraph 2?

4 Reduce the message of each paragraph to a single sentence.

Summarising to a word limit

Biographical extract

Condense the following biographical extract into brief notes, retaining only the essentials of the original (limit: 90 words).

KETCH, JACK (d. 1686), executioner, took office probably in 1663. He seems to have been, or to have become, lamentably inefficient – although he is alleged to have gone on strike for higher fees in 1682. He bungled the beheading of Lord Russell in 1683, defending himself (in a pamphlet which he apparently wrote) on the ground that Russell 'did not dispose himself for receiving the fatal stroke in such a position as was most suitable and that he moved his body'. Two years later there was an appalling scene at Monmouth's execution, when Ketch threw down his axe after three unsuccessful blows, crying 'I can't do it'. The sheriffs compelled him to go on, and it took five blows in all and the use of a knife to sever the head. This professional ineptitude, combined with the part he took in the whipping of Titus Oates, gave him such notoriety that the executioner in 'Punchinello' came to be known as Ketch. He died in November 1686.

Who's Who in History Vol. III C P Hill

Newspaper item

Reorganise and reduce the following newspaper item to produce a report of no more than 180 words. Make careful use of a headline of your own to state the subject of the piece, and sub-headings to label paragraph divisions.

The big squeeze hits boom capital

CARACAS, the brash, dynamic capital of Venezuela, South America's boom state, is growing so fast it is turning into an environmentalist's nightmare.

Caracas has too much of just about everything – too many people, too many cars, too many factories, too much pollution, too much noise – and all are increasing at a frenetic speed.

It also, in a way, has too much money, for the wealth generated by enormous world oil price rises has sparked a consumer boom of near gigantic proportions, heightening the city's already acute problems.

One thing Caracas does not have is space to spread. The city is a spectacular concentration of often sky-scraper-size concrete crammed into a steep-sided, narrow valley.

From east to west it extends some 12 miles while from north to south the valley is not more than three miles wide. The villas of the rich and the shanties of the poor cling to the mountain slopes on both sides.

GIANT JAMS

In the few quiet hours of the night traffic hurtles through the city along a bewildering series of superhighways. The rest of the time it crawls, protesting, along the same superhighways, locked in giant traffic jams.

From above, with the near-perpetual sun highlighting its spectacular setting, and especially at night, when the city lights shine prettily on the valley floor and along the hillsides, Caracas is a beautiful sight.

Down at mid-city street level in the warmth of the afternoon it is a horrifying, petrol-fumey nerve bending place where the car is king and the pedestrian, unconsidered, has to survive as best he can.

The city has a population of at least 2.6 m and it is growing at about six per cent a year.

Underlining this growth rate a recent United Nations study estimated that Caracas would double its population by the end of this century.

ONLY UP

"I don't know where they're all going to fit," said a local businessman. "We've got only one way to spread – up. Up the mountains or straight up in the air."

According to the Urban Planning Ministry about 40 per cent of the total population live in the very poor "ranchos" or shanties which carpet the mountain sides around Caracas and sprout in unexpected clusters in the modern city centre.

Caracas, like most of the capitals of Latin America, suffers from the tendency of the rural poor to migrate to the city in search of wealth.

While Venezuela's oil and other heavy industry is located well away from the capital, Caracas has a lot of light industry, chiefly textiles. The government has a scheme for major investment to decentralise industry and coax people away from the city with the prospect of jobs, but so far things are moving slowly.

The cost of cosmetics

What information does the following article give on:

1 the reason why the cosmetic industry was being badly hit at the time the article was written and why the fall in sales was unexpected?
2 the financial risks involved in producing cosmetics?
3 the new groups of people the industry tried to attract?
4 the new methods of marketing cosmetics and the effect of this?

THE MAKE-UP BUSINESS

Each year, we spend hundreds of millions of pounds on cosmetics and toiletries. Estimates of the total retail value of the British cosmetics market vary, but it is thought to be somewhere in the region of £700,000,000 a year. PAYDAY has been looking at the cosmetics industry and examining the costs and prices of make-up and toilet preparations.

In common with other industries, the make-up business has been faced with difficult trading conditions over the past year or two.

However, this is not what the industry has come to expect. In previous periods of recession, the cosmetics industry was one which traditionally did well. As one of the directors of a cosmetics firm put it, 'women have previously felt that there was only one thing worse than being poor, and that was looking poor'.

This time around the effects of the depression are being felt in the cosmetics world and the major producers are having to fight hard to keep their sales and profits at previous years' levels. Even in usual conditions, the cosmetics business is one of the most competitive industries in the world. In difficult conditions, the fight for market shares becomes even fiercer.

Fragrances

The perfumery side of the business is the one which attracts the highest individual level of consumer expenditure, somewhere in the area of £100,000,000 a year, but it is also the one which is most dangerous from a manufacturer's point of view.

For every product which catches on like Revlon's 'Charlie' range of fragrances, there are many others which do not win lasting favour with the buying public.

Generally, the products at either end of the cosmetics rainbow are maintaining their popularity and market share. The top end of the market, with exclusive brand names and fairly expensive products like Christian Dior and Estee Lauder, and the bottom end, with relatively cheap and cheerful cosmetics and toiletries like Outdoor Girl and Rimmel, have both been doing well. It is in the middle price range that manufacturers and retailers are feeling the pinch.

Men's toiletries

Traditionally concerned just with women and girls, over the past five or six years the cosmetics industry has come to appreciate the enormous market represented by Britain's male population. From aftershave to body lotion, from cologne to talc, the men of Britain have not been slow to welcome the opportunity to make the most of their appearance.

British men spend around £60,000,000 a year on toiletries – or have it spent for them by wives, daughters, sisters or girlfriends!

Catching them young

Over the past few years, the cosmetics industry has concentrated its selling efforts on the 16–24 age group. This is now changing, as manufacturers and retailers concentrate on both the slightly older woman and the much younger girl.

Tinkerbell, a Folkestone cosmetics manufacturer, last month launched a range of beauty preparations for little girls aged between 5 and 11 – including lip salves, lipsticks, talcs, skin creams, and nail varnishes.

Costs and prices

Although the traditional outlets for cosmetics and beauty preparations, the chemists' shops and the beauty counters in department stores, have been saying that the cosmetics business is falling off and becoming much more uncertain, the supermarkets have experienced exactly the reverse.

Nowadays, in stores like Tesco, British Home Stores, Marks & Spencer, and Sainsburys, you can buy make-up and toiletries alongside the baked beans, frozen peas, and catfood. The four groups mentioned have all introduced their own brands of cosmetics.

What price a face?

A recent survey examined the comparative costs of making up a face using different products. To make up a face using Marks & Spencer's fragrance-free items cost £5·94. Using the British Home Stores' 'Eleanor Moore' products, the cost rose to £6·78. The cost using Tesco's 'Cover Girl' cosmetics was £6·14, while the lowest cost of £5·41 was achieved by using Sainsburys' 'Natur' products.

PAYDAY examined the trade and retail prices of some cosmetics for men and women, and the panel gives some examples.

You can see that the retailer's mark-up or gross profit is usually fairly high, ranging from just below 35% to more than 100%. True, the retailer has many and rising costs to meet from his profits and the items with high profit margins are not always the best sellers, but it still appears to be an extremely profitable business.

Facing the next decade

According to cosmetics industry specialists, the look for the 1980s is going to be similar to that in vogue during the 1950s: a well-groomed appearance, elegant and grown-up.

These opinions seem to be confirmed by recent press surveys. Taking a look at the changes over the past 25 years, the IPC group of magazines found that the use of eye shadow had rocketed since 1955. Then, only 5% of women and girls surveyed used eye shadow; nowadays, the proportion has risen to 65%. Similarly, the use of mascara has spread widely; from 12% of women in 1955 to 60% in 1980.

Rouge went out of fashion after its widespread use during the early 1960s, but has now come back as blusher. Face powder fell out of favour as new generations thought it old hat. Now, it is back in fashion and usage levels are rising rapidly.

There are going to be many changes in the cosmetics buying habits of British women and girls, anxious once again to emphasize their feminity. Despite all the past year's trading problems, the cosmetics industry is expecting a bouyant Christmas and a very prosperous New Year.

189

Speed limits

Reproduce the information given below:

1 in the form of an easily read table;
2 by questions and answers.

Do *You* know the speed limits?

Recent surveys have shown that many drivers are unaware of the speed limits that apply to certain types of road. Not only is this dangerous but it can also lead to the motorist losing his licence.

There are five commonly found speed limits: 30, 40, 50, 60 and 70 miles per hour, but not all are signed on the individual roads where they apply.

Speed limits of 30, 40 and 50 mph can be found on any road but they appear mostly in built-up areas. Limits of 40 and 50 mph are always signed and are backed-up with repeater signs.

The 30 mph limit is a special case. Although signs are erected to show where that limit begins, repeater signs are not used to show 30 mph where there is street lighting. This could mean that a motorist driving within a town may not see any speed limit signs. How is he to know that a 30 mph limit applies? The answer is, quite simply, by street lighting. This limit is automatically imposed on all roads with street lighting, including any dual carriageways, so if there are no signs indicating a higher speed limit, the limit is 30 mph.

A change from a lower limit to the national one is indicated by the national speed limit sign: a white circle with a black diagonal.

These national speed limits are 70 mph on dual carriageway roads, including motorways, and 60 mph on single carriageway roads.

These are upper limits set by law and are not necessarily the speed at which a driver can always travel safely, regardless of weather, traffic conditions and time of day. Within the maximum set by law, it is up to each individual to judge what is a safe speed at any point in time and not to exceed that speed. Setting a speed limit at exactly the right level for a particular stretch of road is not easy, and it is necessary for highway authorities to make adjustments from time to time. However, even where a driver feels that a limit has been set at an unreasonably low level, he should still drive within it because he may discover to his cost, and perhaps also that of some innocent bystander, that the limit was chosen for a good, though perhaps not immediately obvious reason.

Department of Transport

The killing of
whales

The killing of whales is, perhaps, one of Mankind's darkest deeds. These magnificent creatures, which have taken millions of years to evolve are being mercilessly hunted and destroyed by Japan, the Soviet Union and about twelve other nations.

5   Modern whaling is big business. Large convoys of ships roam the oceans seeking their prey. These fleets are equipped with sonar, radar, light aircraft, helicopters, fast whale catching vessels, long-range explosive harpoons and factory ships capable of reducing an 80-foot whale to little more than a memory in less than one hour!

10   Whaling is not humane. Although searching for whales is highly sophisticated the actual whale kill is barbaric. The whale is killed by a 160 lb., six-foot-long iron harpoon, shot from a 90 mm cannon. The harpoon strikes the whale at 60 mph and penetrates deep into the body. Seconds later a grenade-like charge in the head of the harpoon explodes inside the whale – causing

15 terrible injuries, but rarely killing the great animal instantly. Some whales have been known to survive for an hour or two before eventually succumbing to the effects of the harpoon.

    In fairness, it must be stated that some whale-catcher skippers will put a second harpoon into a whale to spare it unnecessary suffering, but it would

20 seem that all too many whalers are content to leave their catch to die in its own time rather than 'waste' another harpoon on an animal that is doomed anyway.

    Probably, practically every harpooner goes for an instant kill, without the slightest desire to cause the whale anything other than a quick death. But

25 on the gun platform of a small whale-catcher tossing about in even a fairly moderate sea, it is almost impossible to guarantee just where you are going to hit the whale – if at all.

    However, the fact is that whales are slaughtered to provide products for which there are now plenty of substitutes. Whales are killed for their oil,

30 which finds it way into a vast range of products, but they are killed also for their meat and other portions of the body for which we have found uses. Whale products range from margarine and 'bacon' to steaks, shampoos, perfumes, soaps, lipsticks and other cosmetics, gelatines for confectionery, animal food, shoe polish, floor polish, varnish and paint, fertiliser, glue

35 . . . and many more.

    There is such a lot we still have to learn about the whale family. How is it, for instance, that their vocal sound waves can be detected or 'heard' by another whale of the same species some 200–300 miles away?

    Do we fully understand the physiology which allows certain species of

40 whales – mammals like ourselves – to dive to depths of nearly a mile beneath the ocean surface without apparent discomfort?

    Of course, we realise that whaling cannot cease overnight. Too many jobs and too much capital investment are at stake to do that. However, we do believe that whaling must be quite drastically reduced year by year, with the

45 threatened species rigorously protected by international law – and severe

191

penalties for any infringement. The International Whaling Commission does lay down its own 'laws', but the organisation has no real power and no 'teeth' with which to support its own decisions.

50 Public opinion could bring about a complete ban on the importation of whale oil into the United Kingdom, together with any other products containing any substance obtained from whales. Public opinion could also bring about the reduction in whaling which we believe is so necessary to the survival of the whales into the twenty-first century. Perhaps young people, with our help and guidance, will set an example to their elders by showing

55 their support for our work to save the whales from ultimate extinction at the hand of Man.

Wild Conservation May 1981 Young People's Trust for Endangered Species

Summarise the passage under the following headings:
1 How a whale is killed.
2 Why whales are killed.
3 What should be done about it.

Homework

The following passage is taken from an article on homework. Using only the information in the passage, make a summary consisting of 2 paragraphs as follows:

1 the present situation, and criticisms that are made, regarding homework; and
2 arguments in favour of homework and ways of improving the present situation.

Select the material you need and arrange it in a sensible order within the appropriate paragraph. Write in clear and correct English. Some words and expressions cannot be accurately and economically replaced, but do not copy out long expressions or whole sentences; use your own words as far as possible.

Your whole summary should not exceed 150 words altogether; at the end of your work you must state the exact number of words you have used.

Homework, once associated almost exclusively with the grammar schools, now plays an important role in the lives of children attending comprehensive schools. It is usual for an eleven-year-old to bring home in September a homework timetable, with some notional indication of how much time is to
5 be spent every night on homework, the type and quantity varying from subject to subject. The mathematics teacher sets what might be called traditional homework – so many examples worked to be handed in the day after the homework is set – closely related to classwork. The geography teacher tells the pupils to follow up their own interests and 'get on with their
10 projects', which he will expect to see after half-term. The zealous new teacher sets homework too difficult for the lower half of a mixed-ability group, who react with frustration and non-compliance; the teacher responds by starting to set vague homework tasks: 'Do as much as you can of . . .'

The pupils soon learn that homework, unpredictable in what form it will
15 take and when it will be required of them, is not always central to the work in class. Research would probably reveal large proportions of children who rarely do it. Does this matter? It is arguable that a school controls its children for six hours a day and that should be sufficient at least to impart the basic skills. After four o'clock children should be free to live their own lives
20 and make their own choices. Against this argument several important factors must be weighed. The first is that many parents expect homework to be set, often rating schools by the amount that is given. A second consideration is that homework extends the time available for formal learning. The importance of this will vary, according to the pupil's age and the subject being
25 studied. Physical education is normally conducted without any formal homework (though individual pupils may spend a great deal of their time on it), whereas preparation for external examinations requires a great deal of homework. It is clearly important for schools to encourage children to work on their own, with the support of the teacher withdrawn. This seems a vital
30 preparation for both work and leisure in adult life which will not be learnt if all serious work is done only in the classroom, or if homework is handed in punctually merely under the impulse of fear, or if so much homework is set that the pupil works every night from six o'clock until bedtime. Never-

35 theless, some learning is better done at home on one's own: for example, the revision of French verbs or the first reading of a novel. Much writing may be economically tackled by starting it off in class and completing it for homework. To spend a whole class period writing is to waste a teacher's talents and presence.

40 To argue for homework, however, is not to argue for the present practice. Many of the difficulties which teachers experience flow from the framework set up by the school. An effective homework policy needs to be thought through by a whole staff, preferably in co-operation with the parents. Ideally, an eleven-year-old would receive clear and structured tasks to do at home. Gradually more open-ended homework would become more usual,

45 and, by the time the pupil was sixteen, he or she would be capable of self-directed work. Many of the problems associated with homework arise from the fact that it occurs too frequently. A pupil may be doing two pieces of homework a week in, for example, mathematics, English, general science, and French, and one each in history, geography and religious education. It

50 would be much more helpful to spread these seven subjects not over one week but three. Each subject would be expected to carry one substantial homework in that period. Teachers would then be able to plan and prepare homework in advance and integrate it into their teaching. Pupils would be faced regularly with a solid piece of real work to plan for in their own time,

55 and the problem of two different homework tasks competing for time on the evening of a football match would be reduced when the work was known well in advance. An indirect result might be that pupils began to think for themselves, read more than merely the set books, and tried to express individual opinions.

London University *Paper 1*

Choosing a job

The following passage is based on an article about leaving school. Using only the information given in the passage, write a summary in 2 paragraphs of:

1 the things which influence young people in choosing a job; and
2 the difficulties faced by young people as they go to work for the first time.

You should not attempt to summarise everything there is in the passage, but select from it only the material you need for your two paragraphs. Write in clear, concise English and use your own words as far as possible, although you may retain words and brief expressions which cannot be accurately or economically replaced. Your summary should not exceed 135 words altogether and at the end you must state accurately the number of words you have used.

As young people approach the time to leave school, they spend more and more time thinking and talking about what they will choose as a job or a career. Their choice switches rapidly from one occupation to another when they are still in their early years but as they grow older they look at the situ-
5   ation more realistically and examine critically the opportunities for employment – particularly within the area where they already live.

After studying more than 1,600 school leavers, one research worker found that roughly three quarters of the children settled down in a job only after having changed their ideas very often about what they wanted to do. Many
10   began with fanciful notions about work but in the end their decisions about employment were based on a realisation of what their physical and mental abilities would allow them to do. Once at work the dreams have to cease. Young people find the din of clattering machines, the dirt of lathes, and the frenzy of the typing-pool or workshop quite different from the atmosphere
15   they knew at school; moreover, foremen are usually less tolerant about errors and much more impatient than the strictest teacher.

Very often school leavers follow in the steps of parents or other respected relatives; if nursing or train-driving runs in the family, the young person may well have hopes of becoming a nurse or train-driver. What the adolescent
20   often misses, as he condescendingly watches his tired parents slumped in armchairs in front of the television set in the evening, is the fact that earning a living requires considerable physical or mental effort, but he soon finds that the first job – nursing, train-driving, or some other longed-for career – is exhausting.

25   It is useful for young people to watch a craftsman at work or to see the conditions in an office before making up their minds about a career to follow. A few schools arrange visits to help young people reach a decision and an interest or ability in certain subjects can be matched sometimes against the demands of a particular job. The immediate rewards of work,
30   in the form of a weekly pay-packet or monthly salary, need to be weighed up against long-term opportunities for promotion and work-satisfaction.

The first day at work is often marked by a strong feeling of isolation; old friends are no longer there to lend their support and all the occasions to use

35

40

45

one's initiative, so carefully nurtured at school, are replaced by the demand to conform and become part of a team whose aims are decided by others who may be very remote. Experiments are often discouraged lest the plant or office grinds to a halt; mistakes at work are seen not as part of a natural process of learning but as carelessness which jeopardises the whole factory or business. Most young people seem prepared to accept the idea of a lifetime of such hardships, provided they can feel sure that their jobs will not be threatened by redundancy and offer security. Because retirement seems so distant a prospect, pension rights play a less prominent part in choosing a career but some far-seeing young people take them into account. Facilities for sport, recreation, dancing, outings, and cheap purchases through the firm's social club are additional attractions to balance against the burdens of further study in order to gain qualifications and the lack of status a young newcomer to work often finds. It is not at all easy to exchange the position of prefect, first-eleven captain, or leading actor in the drama society at school for that of junior clerk, apprentice, or student-nurse.

London University *Paper I*

Making friends

The following passage is based on an article which discussed friendship. Using only the information in the passage, make a summary consisting of 2 paragraphs as follows:

1 factors which influence the way friendships are made; and
2 characteristics considered important in friendship.

Select the material you need and arrange it in a sensible order within the appropriate paragraph. Write in clear and correct English. Some words and expressions cannot be accurately and economically replaced, but do not copy out long expressions or whole sentences; use you own words as far as possible.

Your whole summary should not exceed 140 words altogether; at the end of your work you must state the exact number of words you have used.

What do people mean when they talk about 'a friend'? From a recent survey it emerged that men and women often held very different views about friendship. It was also clear that working-class views varied considerably from those of the middle class. In working-class communities in the south of
5 England acts of friendship came most frequently from relatives, with the main duty of neighbours being to keep themselves to themselves. Nevertheless, the needs of the lonely old person or the mother with young children often demanded – and received – a helping hand from those living next door, aid that was rarely refused. The middle classes preferred to maintain friend-
10 ships they had made at school or university rather than make new ones, probably because of common interests or shared experiences. It was noticeable, too, that those who were in their teens placed their emphasis on qualities of friendship markedly different from those suggested by both men and women only ten years older.
15 The view of 'a friend' most commonly held by women was 'someone I can trust'. To be able to trust a person meant one of three things. Very occasionally it meant being able to talk easily with someone else about financial matters that were strictly private. More often it meant being prepared to discuss emotional and personal matters: 'She's more like a sister to me – we
20 talk about everything to each other' (*Wife of a commercial traveller*). Usually, however, it meant being able to confide secret information in the certain knowledge that it would never be revealed to anyone else: 'She keeps everything I tell her to herself; she's not the sort to let the whole world know my business' (*Wife of a factory worker*). Women who lived in small houses
25 huddled together in long terraces in towns were more ready to trust their friends with such confidential, private information than those who spent their days in the larger, more lonely, detached houses in the suburbs.
Men preferred the definition of 'a friend' as 'someone I can call on for help'. Sometimes they merely meant someone from whom they could borrow
30 tools or on whom they could rely completely in moments of personal crisis, such as illness in the family, or an accident, or a bereavement. Usually the definition was left vague: 'I would say a friend was one who was there to help you when you needed help' (*Photographer*). Friendship had to be

197

35 earned and was based on experience spread over a period of time, often as long as five years or more. A single act of betrayal was enough for a friendship to be broken once and for all; it was really as fragile as a flower which took years to cultivate but which could be cut down by a single night's frost.

Some 20 per cent of those questioned emphasised the pleasure that friendship gave them; 'Close friends are those you like being with, whose company
40 you enjoy' (*Warehouseman*); 'They are those you can talk to easily, with views similar to your own' (*Accountant*). Others shared the attitude that a friend was 'someone you don't have to put on an act for'. In certain parts of the country, particularly in the north, they always expected to receive a warm welcome, even when they entered each other's houses unannounced.

45 The survey finally showed that the young sometimes used friendship to enhance their own status within the community; the adolescent girl wanted to be envied by her peers as she walked hand-in-hand with her new boyfriend; the teenage boy asserted his manhood by an exaggerated demonstration of friendship with his 'mates' in the football team. Such
50 displays sprang from a fundamental feeling of personal insecurity and a deep longing to be accepted by others. Whatever the basis on which friendship is formed, it is clear that it both expresses and meets a deep human need.

London University *Paper I*

Processes

Processes – describing a sequence of operations or actions – can be extremely difficult to express precisely.

For example, consider the following account of a simple childhood game: conkers. To those who can recall the game, the opening summary seems a sufficient outline. For someone who does not know a conker from a marble, far more detail is necessary: description that is carefully ordered (equipment, preliminaries, method) and even diagrams to make certain instructions clear.

Conkers

Conkers is a popular game with British children. Two players each have a 'conker' threaded on a knotted string. Players take alternate hits at their opponent's conker and the game is won when one player destroys the other's conker.

The conkers   The game is usually played with nuts from the horsechestnut tree, but is sometimes played with hazelnuts (often called 'cobnuts').

When preparing their conkers, players make a hole through the centre with a sharp instrument such as a meat skewer or a compass or a pair of geometry dividers. Many players then harden their conkers by soaking them in vinegar or salt and water and/or baking them for about half an hour. Excellent conkers are obtained by storing them in the dark for a year.

When the conker is ready, a strong piece of string or a bootlace is threaded through the hole and knotted at one end. The string should be long enough for about 9in to hang down after it is wrapped once or twice around the hand.

The game   Players take alternate hits at their opponent's conker.

The player whose conker is to be hit first, holds his conker as shown (**a**) – with the string wrapped around his hand. He must adjust the height of his hand to suit his opponent, and must then keep his conker perfectly still for the hit.

The striker takes his conker in one hand and holds the opposite end of his string in the other hand (**b**). For the strike, he first draws the conker back and then releases it in a fast swinging motion in the direction of his opponent's conker (**c**).

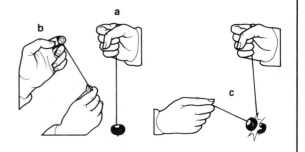

If the striker misses his opponent's conker he is allowed a maximum of two further attempts to make a hit. If the players' strings tangle, the first player to call 'strings' can claim an extra shot.

Play continues until one of the conkers is destroyed – ie until no part of it remains on the string.

Scoring   Conkers are usually described according to the number of victories won with them – eg a 'oner', 'fiver', 'seventy-fiver'.

A conker adds one to its title each time it destroys a conker that has never won a game. A conker that defeats a conker with previous wins claims one for defeating it plus all the defeated conker's wins – so a 'fiver' that defeats another 'fiver' becomes an 'elevener'.

The Way to Play The Diagram Group

For the sake of brevity and clear step-by-step advice, many processes tend to be expressed disjointedly (or even in deliberate note form). To some extent this effect is unavoidable given the imperatives (must . . . have to . . .) and cautionary notes (do not . . . never . . . ensure, etc.) that certain instructions need. Yet processes can be made to read more fluently by varied use of sequence words (firstly, then, when, next, finally, etc.), at the same time assisting your reader's grasp of the order of events.

Bake your own bread

In this example, rewrite the sentences of the following recipe to produce a more fluent paragraph of instructions in sequence.

Ingredients

1 lb. wholemeal flour
1 dessert spoon vegetable oil
1 teaspoon salt
$\frac{1}{2}$ oz. fresh yeast
1 teaspoon sugar
$\frac{1}{2}$ pt. warm water ($\frac{1}{4}$ pt. boiling, $\frac{1}{4}$ pt. cold)

SPRINKLE sugar on to yeast and stir gently. Leave it to liquefy while you add salt and oil to flour. Add warm water to liquefied yeast. Now add the yeast mixture to your flour. Mix well. Knead and shape. Put dough into well-greased 2 lb. loaf tin. Cover with a clean cloth and leave dough to rise in warm place for 15–30 minutes depending on temperature. Bake in oven at 400° F (Mark 6) for 15 minutes then at 350° F (Mark 4) for about another 15 minutes. Remove loaf from tin and turn it upside down. Tap bottom of loaf with knuckles. It should sound hollow. If not, bake for a little longer.

Exercises

1 Modelling your approach on the extract above on conkers, choose one game from each of the following two lists and describe the process involved. First attempts will need a partner's assistance to test for accuracy and inclusiveness.

   a) snap, hopscotch, hide and seek, blind man's buff, an egg and spoon race, or another childhood game of your own choice

   b) Scrabble, pool, pinball, darts (501)

(Divide the process into basic stages first: requirements, method of play, ending.)

2 Aiming to amuse, yet still following the process involved, imagine yourself as an alien trying to describe one of these strange sports to a friend:
fishing, tennis, golf, lacrosse, cricket, rugby

3 Give exact instructions to a friend who is to travel by public transport from school to your home.

4 Explain how you would approach one of these tasks:

   a) decorating a room

   b) arranging a continental holiday for your family, or a party for your friends at home

   c) buying a second-hand car/bicycle or motor bike

   d) organising a wedding

(Make careful notes on the order of essential stages before describing your opinion of the process in full.)

5 Give clear instructions for one of the following:

   a) caring for a record collection (storage and playing)

   b) applying facial make-up (face, eyes and lips)

   c) preparing a breakfast of fresh orange juice, scrambled egg on toast, and a pot of tea

   d) operating a cassette tape recorder

   e) using a cheque book and cheque card (to obtain money and goods)

Education in Britain

Translate the following diagram into a description of the process of education in Britain.

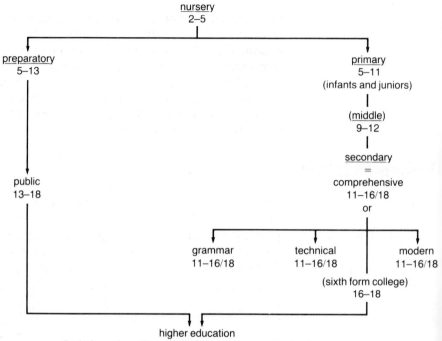

Skills – leaving school

Letters

Many people are nervous when writing letters, often because they are afraid of using the wrong form. It is similar to the anxiety some people have of wearing the wrong type of clothes for a particular occasion. The comparison with clothes is a useful one to remember for, just as casual clothes are acceptable for certain situations, and formal clothes are acceptable on other occasions, so the form and content of letters may be casual or formal according to the situation. Remember: **do not use the informal style and layout for formal or business letters**.

Informal letters

Informal letters are letters to friends and close acquaintances. It is usual to include your address, indented, at the top right with the date beneath it. The greeting is Dear . . . or, if appropriate, something more affectionate. The content and the wording of the letter should be as natural as possible (see Register) and appropriate to the situation, e.g.

> 123, Sandown Road,
> Racecar AN4 3TR
> 14th October, 1983
>
> Dear Jennie,
>
> Thanks a lot for your present of the E.N.T.'s "Gargle, Gurgle, Gasp." It's one of my top 5 favourite albums and now I have got 4 of them. Who told you this was one of the missing ones? I bet it was Tony. Sorry you couldn't be at the party, but I understand why you could not manage it. We had a great time and everybody enjoyed themselves.
>
> Hope to see you soon
> Pat

Formal or business letters

The purpose of the formal letter is to give or ask for information. It should make its point clearly and precisely and all colloquial or slang terms should be excluded. Although many firms and individuals have printed paper with a variety of styles of heading, there is a generally accepted form of layout. An example is given below with notes.

---

(1) 123, Wyndham Road,
Parvenu,
Middlesex, ME9 7AB
(2) 18th December, 1983

(3) The Personnel Manager,
Green Bros. Ltd.,
Saxon Street,
Hants. HE9 8UF

(4) Dear Sir,

(5) <u>Application for Trainee Post</u>

(6)   I have seen your advertisement in today's paper asking for applications for the post of Trainee Buyer. As I have the qualifications you stipulate and am seeking a career in Buying, I would be grateful if you would send me the application forms.

(7) Yours faithfully,
Diane Pattwell

---

1 Give your full address on the top right, indenting it.

2 Do not forget the date. It is an important way of singling out a letter from a number on the topic. Align it underneath the start of the first word of the first line of your address.

3 Always include the name and address of the addressee, i.e. the person to whom the letter is sent. If a copy of the letter is kept by you it makes clear to whom it was sent. Normally the name and address are not indented. It is also not unusual to find this part at the top of the letter on the left-hand side immediately before the greeting.

4 The usual greeting, if the name of the recipient is not known, is *Dear Sir,* (note the capital letters and comma).

5 It is often helpful to give a centre heading indicating the general topic of the letter.

6 The body of the letter:
   a) Start it on the line below the title. If there is no title start on the line below the greeting and after the comma.
   b) Set out the facts clearly and precisely. Do not use chatty or colloquial language. Do not forget to use paragraphs if they are necessary.
   c) Try to avoid common jargon and cliches, e.g. 'Yours of the 12th ult. to hand' or 'I am in receipt of'.

7 The signing-off or subscription.
   If the greeting is *Dear Sir* sign off with *Yours faithfully.* If the greeting is by name, e.g. *Dear Ms Pringle,* sign off with *Yours sincerely.*
   Note the capital Y but the small f or s.

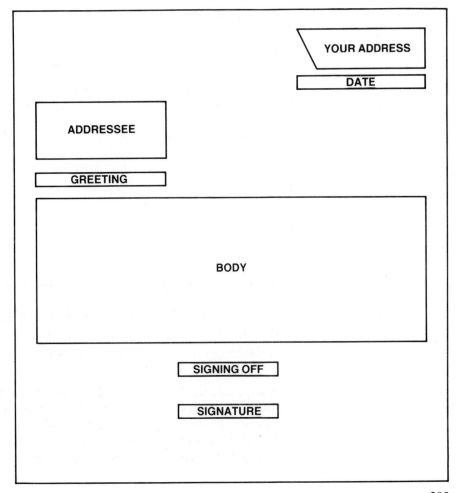

The Bank of England

Using the relevant parts of the information given below, what advice would you give to the following school leavers who were thinking of applying for a position in the Bank of England? Write a friendly letter to each of them. (All four are close relatives.)

1 Janet White, 16 years, lives in outer London – has 'O' level English Language and likes taking part in sport.

2 Bill Ferguson, 18 years, lives in small remote Scottish village – has five 'O' levels including Maths and English and is expected to pass three 'A' levels – has built his own small computer

3 Susan French, 18 years, lives thirty miles from London – has five 'O' levels, two 'A' levels and has completed a commercial course in typing and shorthand – likes the theatre

4 John Matthews, 16 years – lives in London – no 'O' levels but awaiting CSE results – has plenty of initiative and wants to travel – ambitious

The Bank of England

Background

The Bank of England is the central bank of the United Kingdom, at the hub of the country's financial life. It is banker to the Government and the Government's adviser on monetary and financial affairs; banker to the principal UK banks and to many overseas central banks; manager of the national debt; registrar of government stocks; the note issuing authority; and the Government's agent in a number of operations.

Types of career offered

A wide variety of career opportunities (including computer operating and programming).

Locations of employment

The majority of the banking staff work in the City of London, although some are employed at the Bank's eight branches outside London and at the printing works in Essex.

Training courses/Minimum age/Qualifications required

Banking staff scale 2: entry is open to men and women who have obtained sufficient subjects at GCE 'O' level, including mathematics and English language, to prove a sound general education. In addition, they must have completed a full 'A' level course in at least two academic subjects. In the selection of candidates, considerable weight is attached to all-round ability, personality and sense of responsibility.

All new entrants attend a short induction course designed to give them a broad picture of the activities of the Bank of England. This is followed by practical experience in a number of departments, the choice and sequence depending on vacancies, and the qualifications, aptitudes and preferences of the individual. This practical training is accompanied, at intervals, by development courses aimed at consolidating and expanding the knowledge already gained. Courses on specialised skills are run as necessary. Throughout, every effort is made to ensure that staff are given the right experience and opportunity to develop their potential to the full.

Those showing the necessary ability may be selected for the advanced training scheme, which ensures that their career paths are adjusted to yield the right balance of experience, responsibility and training to equip them for early promotion to supervisory and administrative posts.

Banking staff scale 1: entry is open to men and women aged 16 and over, who have studied GCE 'O' level in a wide range of academic subjects. Those who have achieved, or hope to achieve, a high standard in the CSE are also accepted. Although generally employed on the more straightforward work, scale 1 staff undertake a wide range of jobs: for example, the coding of cables, responsibility for departmental information and records, or preparing work for the Bank's computers. All necessary training is given within the Bank.

Computer staff: A limited number of junior operators and junior programmers are recruited annually. The entry requirements are similar to those for Banking staff scale 2 but candidates must also show an aptitude for this type of work. Full training is normally given.

Typing and secretarial staff: Secretaries would normally be recruited as scale 2 staff and typists as scale 1, and in addition to meeting the appropriate academic qualifications must have typing and (in the case of secretaries) shorthand experience.

Further study: Staff who wish to progress to the administrative ranks in the Bank must complete the HNC (or in the case of graduates a one year post graduate diploma) in business or financial studies. There is provision for part-time day release for those studying these courses.

Employee welfare

Pension and widows' benefits are provided which are non-contributory. Other amenities include generous leave entitlements, assistance with house purchase, interest free loans for season tickets, subsidised meals and refreshments, and excellent sports and social facilities. The Bank has a superbly equipped sports centre on a thirty-eight acre site at Roehampton in south west London.

Applications by form and by letter

1 Application forms

1 Always read the forms through before filling them in.
2 If the sections of the form are numbered, write down the numbers and do a rough draft of the information you are to give.
3 Alternatively, if you can photocopy the forms, do so and complete the copy.
4 Write or type clearly.
5 If you want to give more information than there is room for, write a covering letter.
6 When you have completed the form, check it over.

2 Letters of application

If you have to write a letter of application, remember that the employer will judge you by what you write and how you write it.

1 Use the formal layout for the letter (cf. p. 204) and adopt the correct register (cf. p. 16).
2 Do a draft copy.
3 Write or type clearly.
4 Set out the information in an orderly, logical way so that the employer can readily take in the details.
5 Include:
   a) information on yourself (see Curriculum Vitae on p. 209)
   b) reasons why the job interests you
   c) reasons why you think you are particularly suited for the job.
6 Check what you have written for spelling, grammar and punctuation mistakes.
7 Keep a copy of what you have written.

3 Constructing a curriculum vitae

A curriculum vitae is a summary of the relevant information about yourself. The following should be a helpful outline:

1 *Personal details*
   a) name and address, telephone number
   b) date and place of birth

   2 *Education*
   a) schools attended and dates
   b) public examinations taken and results
   c) public examinations taken for which you have not yet had results
   d) public examinations to be taken in the near future
   e) other achievements and positions of responsibility

3 *Experience*
   details of full- and part-time employment, including holiday jobs

4 *Other information*
      a) your hobbies and interests
      b) membership of clubs and organisations

5 *References*
      a) copies of any written references or reports which you have
      b) names of people willing to act as referees, that is, to provide a reference for you

4 Preparation for interview

You should be prepared to discuss any of the details you have provided on the form or in the letter. Prepare yourself adequately if you are invited to an interview. Even if you do not get the job, keep all the details relating to your application and after the interview write down, for future reference, the questions you were asked and particularly those that you found difficult.

Exercises

1 Write out a letter of application to the employer whose details are given on p. 207.

2 Construct a curriculum vitae for:
   a) yourself
   b) a member of your family
   c) a close friend
   d) a famous person you admire

Spoken English

Spoken English is the most common type of English. For many people it is the only form of English they use after leaving school. In spite of this, examination bodies have been reluctant to include it in examinations in English Language. However, this is changing and there has been a steady increase in the number of examinations including an oral element.

Experience has shown that fluency in the spoken language can be learned and examinations can play an important part in ensuring that it is.

Individual performance

Individual performances fall into two categories: the talk and the reading.

Prepared talks

The examination demands that you talk on a subject in which you are interested. You should speak for at least five minutes and be prepared to answer questions afterwards. You are allowed to use visual and aural aids.

Preparation

The most important task is to choose the right topic. Choose a topic about which you know a great deal and which you feel will interest or excite your audience.

Once you have chosen your subject, consider the aspects you wish to cover. Notice how, in the following example, ideas radiate from the central topic:

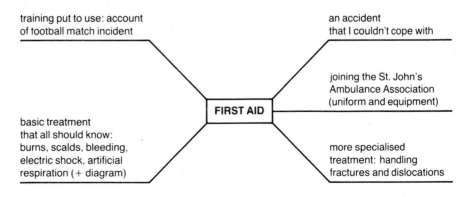

Work out similar diagrams for one of the following:

Squash, Camping, Stamp collecting, Kites, Fishing, Cameras, Chess, Netball

The ideas are at present in no particular order. Your next task will be to arrange the ideas in their most effective order. For example, for the First Aid topic, the most effective order might be:

1 An accident I couldn't cope with
2 Joining St John's Ambulance Association
3 Basic treatment
4 More specialised treatments
5 Training put to use

A good talk will have an easily recognisable shape and structure. The topic will be *introduced*, the major points *developed* through the meat of the talk and the *conclusion* should be organised, not left to chance.

The *introduction* should last no more than half a minute during which the audience should be told what the talk is about. It might include some of your views on the topic and the reasons why you chose it.

The *development* of your topic should take about four minutes. In this section you will be expected to expand on the ideas and fill out the details mentioned in your introduction. The ideas and information should be presented in a logical, ordered sequence. Using a visual aid often helps logical development by reminding you of the sequence you wish to follow. If your topic contains specialised terms then a diagram or picture will complete the sense of your spoken explanation. Indeed if your talk is heavily technical or obviously very practical in nature then absence of an appropriate visual aid can be a great disadvantage.

Your *conclusion* should also be planned, not just a matter of: 'well that's it. Any questions?' It should last about half a minute and should attempt to sum up your ideas without repeating earlier details.

The final stage in preparation is to reduce your speech to note headings written on a postcard. This will remind you of the sequence of your speech and at the same time, prevent you from merely reading out your notes.

A final plan for a talk on Fishing might be:

Heading	Points	Visual aids
Introduction First experiences	childhood pursuit of sticklebacks holiday mackerel fishing fishing trips with brother	
Development Becoming interested/ buying equipment	first rod and reel rod and reel used now other angling essentials	hold up both rods and contrast display waders and maggots to amuse show artificial flies
The enjoyment	favourite fishing spot peace and relaxation excitement of the catch	scale diagram of my largest fish
The hazards	weather, trespassing and bailiffs	
Conclusion Ambition	to land a sizeable pike describe recent "near miss"	scale diagram of UK record pike, deliberately dwarfing previous diagram

Exercises

Plan a talk on the above lines on one of the following subjects:

Playing a musical instrument; Life saving; Pottery; Snooker; Hiking; the Eye; Modern Aircraft; Darts; Motor Bicycles; Hockey; Poisonous Plants; Eclipses; Nutrition and Diet; Video Machines; Hair Styles; How a Record is made; Cosmetics.

Performance

Such a thorough preparation will give you the confidence to be committed to your subject and your audience.

1 Be enthusiastic, especially at the beginning, in order to gain their immediate attention and hold their interest.

2 Be warm and friendly – you are talking to your fellow pupils. If you wish to share your experience with your audience, look at them and make your talk meaningful to each of them.

3 Speak clearly and audibly ensuring that even those furthest away can hear you easily.

4 Give special weight to the important details or ideas and pause to allow your audience to reflect upon what you have said.

5 Don't attempt to learn your talk by heart for two reasons: firstly, your delivery will be flat and wooden; and secondly, if you forget any details or the order in which they arise, you will quickly lose confidence and possibly even dry up altogether.

6 When you have finished speaking you should be ready to answer some questions. These questions will usually fall into two categories:
   a) those which require you to clarify something in your talk by re-explaining it, e.g. 'How does a certain part of a machine work?';
   b) those which require you to justify your choice of topic or the way you treated it, e.g. '*Why* did you choose to speak to us today on . . .?' 'and '*What* is the point of future research into . . .?'

You will be assessed on the way you handle these questions and the way you develop your answers. So take your time, answer clearly and honestly and if your preparation has been thorough, you will answer with confidence.

Prepared reading

Reading is generally assessed in two ways:

1 You will be asked to read a prepared passage of suitable length from a novel, play or poem. (A passage of about 500 words will be sufficient.)

2 The examiner or teacher will choose a passage from your book and after a few minutes' preparation, you will be asked to read it out.

Preparation

Good readings demand a thorough preparation. Whether you or your teacher select the passage from your chosen book, the preparation will be essentially the same. You should have read the complete book thoughtfully and methodically to gain the most thorough understanding of its meaning, its characters and its plot.

You should choose a passage that you enjoy and is essential to the development of plot, theme or character. In order to exhibit the widest range of your reading skills, it is wise to choose a passage which contains both dialogue and narration or description. If you have chosen a play or a poem you must ensure it is of a sufficient length. You could, of course, choose more than one poem by the same poet or on the same theme; or choose more than one extract from a play, perhaps concentrating on a single character. But whatever you choose there should be sound reasons for your choice. You may have to justify your choice in answering questions when you have finished.

You must now spend some time studying the passage in detail.
1 Should it be read quickly or slowly?
2 Does the pace alter during the passage?
3 Which words or phrases need special emphasis?
4 Where do the pauses occur?
5 Practise your interpretation a number of times. Have you captured the atmosphere of the passage and brought the words to life?
6 Remember if your extract contains dialogue that you should pay special attention to the words indicating the tone and volume of the voice to be used, especially at the end of the passage. Try to vary your voice for different characters.

Performance

Begin your reading by introducing the book and give the context of the chosen passage so that the audience may more fully respond to the reading. Set the scene and give a brief sketch of the relevant characters. In your reading you should aim to show that you can fully communicate the author's meaning by paying due attention to tone, pace and emphasis and by bringing out the significance of character, incident and feeling. A more dramatic use of your voice will help to display the range of reading skills. Share the experience by looking regularly at your audience at appropriate pauses in the reading.

Group performance

A group performance is an activity in which two or more candidates are involved; it covers discussion, debate, conversation and role play.

Discussions

A discussion is a friendly exchange of ideas on a given topic. In a discussion you need to show your ability to listen to the ideas of others, to assess what has been said, and to put forward your point of view. Unmannerly interruptions should be avoided and your remarks should be as constructive as possible. Base your opinions on facts, knowledge or experience.

Topics

The topics given, or which you choose, should cover matters about which you are in a position to have an opinion or belief. In order for the discussion to develop, the topic should be open to points of view, e.g. Corporal/Capital Punishment, Censorship, Euthanasia, Racial Discrimination, Ulster, Politics and Sports, Apartheid, The Generation Gap, Youth Unemployment, Television Violence, Christian Unity, The Monarchy, Immigration, The School Curriculum, The Influence of Advertising, Pop Culture, Jokes and Humour.

These topics are broadly based. It is sometimes better to focus on a specific issue, e.g. 'Should we restore the death penalty for terrorism?'

When you have chosen your topic make certain you have time to prepare your ideas thoroughly. You should then meet as a group and clarify your initial points of view for the benefit of each other. If you find you all have similar attitudes and sympathies it is sometimes helpful for one of the group to play the devil's advocate. That is, one of the group deliberately supports views which he doesn't believe and so ensures that a genuine discussion can take place. Finally, each member of the group should research the topic thoroughly, discovering relevant and up-to-date facts and figures so that he/she can make a significant contribution to the discussions.

Performance

For the performance it is better to be seated in an arc facing your audience.

The discussion will begin by either one selected member making introductory remarks to which the rest respond or by each member making, or sometimes reading, an opening statement and the discussion arising out of the conflicts in those remarks.

In order to do well in a discussion you should be able to demonstrate the following skills:

1 a clear understanding of the topic under discussion
2 the ability to speak clearly and articulately
3 the ability to argue logically and coherently
4 the ability to listen sympathetically and attentively to the ideas of others
5 the ability to introduce new ideas and perhaps change the direction of the discussion
6 the ability to introduce and encourage the more reluctant members of the group to make their contribution.

Debates

A debate is an organised discussion in which opposing views are argued.

There are two opposing teams, each having two members, and a chairman. The teams are presented with a topic, similar to those used in a group discussion, and each team puts forward its point of view as clearly and convincingly as possible.

This topic or statement is called the Motion. The speakers who agree with the motion, who speak *for* the motion are called the Proposers; those who disagree, who speak *against* the motion are called the Opposers.

In order to win the debate each team has to convince the majority of the audience (often called the House) of the validity and correctness of its views. At the end of the debate a vote is taken. If the majority is in agreement with the motion, then the motion is carried; if the majority disagrees, the motion is defeated. In case of a tie, the chairman has the casting vote.

Organisation

The rules for conducting a debate are much more formal and structured than in a group discussion. Everything follows a set order and the chairman is elected to ensure it does.

A typical debate may be organised on the following lines:

1 The chairman introduces the motion and both the speakers for and against the motion. He invites the first proposer to argue his case.
2 The first proposer states his views.
3 The chairman thanks him and calls upon the first speaker in opposition to state his case.
4 The first opposer states his case and may refute the arguments of the first speaker.
5 The chairman then invites the other two speakers to present their arguments in turn. When they have finished, he invites comments and questions from the audience.
6 The questions should be directed through the chairman to the speakers.
7 The chairman will then ask a member of the opposition to sum up their arguments.
8 The chairman will ask one of the proposers to sum up their arguments.
9 The chairman thanks all the speakers and calls for a vote on the motion. He will announce the number in favour, and the number against.
10 The chairman will declare the motion carried or defeated.

Your preparation for a debate should be at least as thorough as your preparation for a group discussion. You and your partner must research the subject thoroughly. You must decide who is presenting which arguments and upon the most effective order in which they should be presented.

In your research you should also try to anticipate the arguments put forward by your opposition. This will enable you to answer their points more fluently and confidently.

Remember also to take notes during the debate to ensure that you refute whatever points are made against you. The questions will generally require you to develop your point of view or clarify something in your speech. When responding to a question stand and address yourself politely and confidently to your questioner.

Assessment

As in the discussion you will be expected to show an understanding of the topic, an ability to speak clearly and articulately and an ability to argue logically and convincingly. Furthermore, you will have to show evidence of careful and attentive listening to the view of your opponents by the way you fluently and logically refute their arguments both during the debate and at the summing up.

Conversations

A conversation is a friendly exchange of views. It differs from a discussion in that it is more spontaneous and limited in scope. Topics or issues in conversation tend to be restricted to the immediate concerns of the speakers.

Conversations usually take place between people you trust, your family and your friends. This, however, does not mean that conversations cannot become heated and develop into arguments. e.g.

1 You wish to leave school. You have a chance of a job and wish to take it. Your father wishes you to continue full-time education and possibly go to university.
2 You receive a poor end of term report. You take it to your mother first and try to get round her. She demands you show it to your father. You present your father with your report.

Role play

Role play (particularly in conversations or interviews) is a much more organised activity. Generally speaking, you are given a situation and you are asked to take the role of one of the people involved. You can prepare for the situation, but not always fully. It is necessary to consider thoroughly and from all possible angles the information you have been given. This will help you in what you want to say, but, as you cannot be certain what the other characters are going to say, you have to listen carefully, respond to what has been said, and be willing to discard what you have prepared. Role play in interviews is particularly good practice for the real thing.

In the following situations each part should be taken by a different person and the characteristics of such a person (e.g. speech, attitude, opinion, belief) should be portrayed.

1 You and a friend are looking for a newspaper shop in an area unknown to you. You ask an elderly person directions. That person turns out to be partially deaf.

2 You and at least two of your friends have been found out of school during school hours in a cafe which is out of bounds. The Headteacher interviews all three of you with the result that one is given a warning, one is given a more severe punishment, the third is let off.

3 Telephone conversations:
   a) booking a seat at a pop concert;
   b) asking for information from a travel agent regarding holidays;
   c) apologising to a friend because you have lost his/her favourite record.

4 Conversation between a parent and a door-to-door salesman of one of the following:

   encyclopaedias; home insulation; cosmetics; raffle tickets

Index

Index of extracts

Acknowledgements

We are grateful to the following for permission to reproduce copyright material:

Edward Arnold Ltd for an extract from *Who's Who in History* vol III by C. P. Hill; E. J. Arnold Ltd for an extract from Sid Chaplin's 'The Bachelor Uncle' as in *A Few Words* ed. A. Bradley; The Associated Examining Board for questions from pprs 2, 3 & Chief Examiner's comments from *English Language Examination* (069–1980) copies of this & other recent past papers may be purchased from the Board's Publications Dept; Associated Lancashire Schools Examining Board for questions & diagram ppr 1 *16+ Eng. Lang. Examination* 1974; Basic Books Inc for poem 'First Frost' by Andrei Voznesensky from *Antiworlds and the Fifth Ace* ed. Patricia Blake & Max Hayward, © 1966 by Basic Books Inc, 1963 by Encounter Ltd; B. T. Batsford Ltd for the extract 'Kibbutzim' from *The Family* by Mary Waddington from Worldwide Series; the author's agents for an extract from *The Tortoise by Candlelight* by Nina Bawden pub Penguins; Blackie & Sons Ltd for an extract from *Rural Planning Problems* by Gordon E. Cherry; Collins Publishers Ltd for an extract from *The Angry Mountain* by Hammond Innes; Andre Deutsch Ltd for an extract from *Jaws* by Peter Benchley; Gerald Duckworth & Co Ltd for an extract from *Injury Time* by Beryl Bainbridge; the author's agents for an extract from *Twice Shy* by Dick Francis; Hodder & Stoughton Ltd for an extract from *Poverty and the Industrial Revolution* by Brian Inglis; Hutchinson Publishing Group Ltd for an extract from *The Pumpkin Eater* by Penelope Mortimer; Joint Matriculation Board for questions from pprs A II & C *Eng. Lang. 'O' Level Examination* June 1980; the author's agents for an extract from *One Tale of Beatrix Potter* by Margaret Lane, pub. Collins; University of London, School Examination Dept for questions from ppr 1 *Eng. Lang. 'O' Level Examination* Jan & June 1980; MacMillan London & Basingstoke Ltd for extracts from *Connections* by James Burke; City of Manchester Art Galleries for an extract from *20 Paintings* by Julian Treuherz; New Directions Publishing Corporation for poem 'The Hunters in the Snow' by William Carlos Williams from *Pictures from Brueghel*, copyright 1962 by William Carlos Williams; author's agents on behalf of the Estate of the late Sonia Brownell Orwell for an extract from *Marrakesh* by George Orwell; Oxford & Cambridge Schools Examination Board for a question from ppr 1 *Eng. Lang. 'O' Level Examination* June 1980; Oxford Delegacy of Local Examinations for a question from ppr II *Eng. Lang. 'O' Level Examination* June 1980; Oxford University Press for poem 'Lake Morning in Autumn' from *Sjambok and Other Poems from Africa* by Douglas Livingstone, © OUP 1964; Pan Books Ltd for an adapted extract from *Funny Amusing and Funny Amazing* by Denys Parsons; Pelham Books Ltd for an extract from *Come Hell or High Water* by C. Francis; Penguin Books for an extract from *The Unprivileged* by Jeremy Seabrook, Copyright Jeremy Seabrook 1967; Robson Books Ltd for poem 'A Kind of Hero' from *Collected Poems 1950/ 1980* by Vernon Scannell; the author's agents for an extract from p 22 *The Royal Hunt of the Sun* by Peter Shaffer, pub Hamish Hamilton Ltd; The Society of Authors on behalf of the Bernard Shaw Estate for an extract from *Arms and the Man*; the Editor of Stand Magazine for an extract from the story 'Drew' by Graham Swift *Stand Magazine* vol 18, No 3; George Weidenfeld & Nicholson Ltd for an extract from *A. J. Wentworth B. A.* by H. Ellis; Vallentine, Mitchell & Co Ltd for an adapted extract from *Ash on a Young Man's Sleeve* by Dannie Abse; the author's agents for an extract from *Black Boy* by Richard Wright, pub Longman Group Ltd (LIB 1970); Young People's Trust for Endangered Species for an extract from article by Cyril Littlewood from p 3 *Wildlife Conservation* No 2, May 1981.

We have unfortunately been unable to trace the copyright holders of the extract 'Conkers' from *The Way to Play*; extract from *The Climbers Fireside Book* by Martyn Berry; and extracts entitled 'Making Friends', 'Choosing a Job', 'Homework'; and 'Buried Treasure' by Roy Norvill from *The Treasure Seekers Treasury* and would appreciate any information which would enable us to do so.

We are grateful to the following for permission to reproduce photographs and other illustrations:

Barnaby's Picture Library, pages 10 (photo Linda Grove), 149 below (photo Leonardo Ferrante), 171 above left (photo Elizabeth Goodwin), above right and below (photo T. K. Erskine); BBC, page 218; Camera Press, page 167 (photo Eamonn McCabe); Ron Chapman, pages 149 above, 171 centre and 216; Greater Manchester Police Traffic Department, *On the Road*, page 174; Richard and Sally Greenhill, page 151; Kunthistorischen Museum, Wien, page 57 (*Hunters in the Snow*, P. Breugel); Manchester City Art Gallery, page 65 (*Winter Scene*, Jan van Goyen); Manchester City Council, Recreational Services Department, page 178; *Manchester Evening News*, page 188; MEPhA, page 9 left (photo Alistair Duncan); from the MGM release *North by North-West*, © Metro-Goldwyn-Mayer Film Company/UIP, page 165; Daniel Meadows, page 9 right; National Girobank's Magazine for Schools, *Payday*, page 189; *Opportunities '79*, New Opportunity Press, page 207; Penzance Town Council, page 164 (*School is Out*, Elizabeth Forbes); 'Rhyl Suncentre' and 'Suncentre' symbols are copyright Rhuddlan Borough Council, and published by the Director of Tourism and Amenities, pages 180–81; *Social Trends 8*, 1977, HMSO, page 179; Sport and General Press Agency, pages 153 and 166; Tate Gallery, page 155 (detail from *Past and Present number 1*, Augustus Egg).

We would be grateful for any information which would help us to trace the copyright holder of the material on pages 176–77.

LONGMAN GROUP UK LIMITED
Longman House
Burnt Mill, Harlow, Essex, CM20 2JE, England
and Associated Companies throughout the World.

© Longman Group Limited 1984

All rights reserved; no part of this publication
may be reproduced, stored in a retrieval system,
or transmitted in any form or by any means, electronic,
mechanical, photocopying, recording or otherwise,
without the prior written permission of the Publishers.

First published 1984
Fourth impression 1987

Set in 10/12pt Times Roman, Linotron 202

Produced by Longman Group (FE) Ltd
Printed in Hong Kong

ISBN 0-582-33084-X